Michael A. Garcia
Attorney at La

INTERSTATE MOVING

CONSUMER PROTECTION AND LEGAL COMPLIANCE GUIDE

"Understand and follow the law, while protecting consumer rights and property."

Michael A. Garcia
Attorney at Law

INTERSTATE MOVING

CONSUMER PROTECTION AND LEGAL COMPLIANCE GUIDE

Michael A. Garcia, Attorney at Law
7676 Hazard Center Drive, 5th Floor
San Diego, California 92108
Tel: (877) 299-0550

www.michaelgarcialaw.com

About the Author

Michael Garcia is an author, regulatory compliance attorney, and consumer protection attorney. His firm specializes in interstate and intrastate transportation law and the representation of household goods moving companies, bus & passenger motorcoaches, and consumers. His practice focuses on regulatory compliance and training, tariff and contract requirements, and consumer protection laws. Mr. Garcia's practice has a strong emphasis on training in order to avoid litigation and regulatory actions by educating motor carriers to operate in compliance with the law and to protect consumers.

Legal Notice

The information contained in this book is designed for informational purposes only. Nothing in this book is designed or intended to constitute legal advice. Federal, state, and local laws and regulations governing the moving industry change frequently and may be interpreted differently by different people. If you need specific legal advice you should consult an attorney specializing in transportation law or a representative from the US DOT.

All products, companies, associations, and/or organizations referenced in this book are included for informational purposes only, and their inclusion should not be understood to be an expressed or implied endorsement of the information contained within or the opinions of the author. The author does not endorse any company, association, or organization referenced in this legal guide.

Preface

This version of the ***INTERSTATE MOVING CONSUMER PROTECTION AND LEGAL COMPLAINCE GUIDE*** is an update to ***MOVING 101*** which was originally published in 2011. This version of the book includes additional consumer protections tips, and updates to the industry regulations.

This book is designed to be a resource for consumers, interstate moving companies, interstate brokers, and those working in the interstate household goods industry. This consumer protection legal guide book includes general information for consumers about interstate moving; including types of estimates, how charges are calculated, delivery windows, filing claims, and much more.

Consumers preparing to move should research their moving company carefully and have a full understanding of the contract for services, how charges are calculated, and what to expect during the move. This guide book is intended to help consumers understand the law, enforce their rights, and protect their property.

Interstate moving companies and brokers should regularly review their operations to ensure full compliance with the safety, economic, and consumer protection regulations. It is important that moving company operators, brokers, and their staffs receive regular training and legal compliance updates. This legal guide provides general legal information relating to various topics of interest to moving companies and brokers and can assist each in taking proactive steps to operate in full compliance with the governing federal regulations.

Included in the appendix of this book is a detailed glossary, a directory of FMCSA offices in each state, a directory of state moving and storage associations, as well as a complete reprint of 49 CFR section 375 *et al* (the consumer protection law governing interstate moving).

Terms and Abbreviations

Motor carrier	A moving company hired to transport household goods.
Consumer shipper	The consumer/customer hiring a moving company to pack, load, and transport household goods.
Broker	A company whom, for compensation, arranges the transportation of property by an authorized interstate motor carrier.
US DOT	United States Department of Transportation
FMCSA	Federal Motor Carrier Safety Administration
USC	United States Code
CFR	Code of Federal Regulations
§	Section
PUC	Public Utilities Commission
STB	Surface Transportation Board
IRS	Internal Revenue Service
EDD	California Employment Development Department
IC	Independent Contractor
FMC	Federal Maritime Commission
BBB	Better Business Bureau
ICC	Interstate Commerce Commission
NVOCC	Non-Vessel Operating Common Carrier

Table of Contents

Chapter 16: Interstate Tariffs

Chapter 17: Interstate Shipping Documents

Chapter 18: Carrier Operations

Chapter 19: Moving Brokers

Chapter 20: Online Lead Providers

Introduction

CHAPTER 1

Generally, full service transportation of household goods can be divided into three types: international, intrastate, and interstate. Each of the types of moves is governed by different laws and regulatory bodies. The information contained in this book concerns **interstate** moves exclusively.

INTERNATIONAL transportation of household goods is the movement of property from an origin in one country to a destination in another country. For example, when a consumer shipper moves from the United States to England. For United States based companies, international moves are regulated by the Federal Maritime Commission. For more information, see www.fmc.gov.

INTRASTATE transportation of household goods is the movement of property from an origin to a destination within the same state. For example, when a shipper moves from Dallas, Texas, to Austin, Texas. Moving companies performing intrastate transportation services must be licensed with that individual state's regulatory body, if any. Generally, the regulatory agencies governing intrastate moving companies are the state Public Utilities Commission (PUC) or state Department of Transportation (DOT). Moving companies should check with their individual state to receive information about the individual licensing requirements.

INTERSTATE transportation of household goods is the movement of property from an origin in one state to a destination in another state. For example, when a shipper moves from San Francisco, California, to Phoenix, Arizona. Interstate moving companies transporting household goods are regulated and licensed by the U.S. Department of Transportation Federal Motor Carrier Safety Administration (FMCSA). More information about the regulatory and licensing requirements may be found at www.fmcsa.dot.gov.

Overview of Interstate Moving

CHAPTER 2

Long distance interstate moving is a complex and expensive undertaking under the best of circumstances. Generally, a consumer will receive the level of service paid for. If a consumer hires a nationally known company they will pay top dollar but will typically receive top of the line service. On the other hand if a consumer has friends who are willing to work for free, are capable and not afraid of exhausting work, then they could rent a truck, pack their own property, have help with the loading and driving, and potentially save thousands of dollars.

For people who do not want to spend top dollar on a nationally known moving company and can't or don't want to do a self-move there are good alternatives. To save money and avoid the hard work consumers can hire a smaller independent moving company, use a broker service, or hire a "you load – they drive" container service. These options are alternatives to expensive top of the line movers or complete do it yourself move. However, consumers using these cost saving services need to have realistic expectations of what is and is not included in the price.

Between the stress of packing, planning, and dealing with the challenges of being uprooted, the last thing consumers need are unexpected hidden charges increasing the cost of the move. To help avoid unexpected charges, a consumer should first understand the types of moving company options available and the cost associated for each.

Consumer protection tip. Read contracts carefully. A contract for moving services contains important legal information and terms concerning how your move will be performed and the total charges you will pay. It is important to read and understand all contracts before signing and never feel pressured to sign any document before you have reviewed it thoroughly.

Generally, there are four categories of long distance interstate moving options. Each category has pros and cons, includes different services, and ranges widely in costs. To help manage the final cost of the move a consumer must understand what is included in the service they are purchasing and how charges are calculated.

Long distance moving service options:

Option 1: Full service all inclusive moving from a nationally known major van line.

The top of the line service in the moving industry is a full service all inclusive move performed by a nationally known major van line. Generally, the major van lines perform quality services with the highest degree of professionalism and will charge a premium for their services. Generally, they will send a representative to the consumer's home to provide an estimate, send a team of movers to do all the packing in the home, transport your goods in top of the line trucks, provide full insurance coverage for any loss or damages, and deliver quickly on a guaranteed date. The nationally known major van line is a good choice for consumers who don't want to lift a finger during their move, receive white glove services, and don't mind paying a premium price.

Option 2: Regional independent moving company and/or moving broker offering *á la carte* services at discounted pricing.

An alternative to hiring a nationally known major van line is to hire a regional independent moving company or use the services of a moving broker working with a network smaller independent regional moving companies. Many of the regional independent moving companies in the broker's network offer *á la carte* moving services. Typically moving brokers provide written estimates based upon a specific list of *á la carte* moving services and items to be moved. Consumers can choose to save money by selecting the service options they want. For example a consumer may wish to choose to perform their own packing, or select the longer ground delivery window instead of an expedited or guaranteed delivery service option. Services are generally offered at a lower cost since the consumer may choose to do some of the work themselves, the broker searches its network for a moving company who has availability on that date, and the property would be consolidated with other shipments on the same truck for transport.

Using the services of a regional independent moving company from a moving broker's network can result in great cost savings. However, consumers need to be aware that prices are quoted based upon a specific list of services. Any deviation or additions to the services ordered can result in price increases – sometimes dramatic price increases. For example, a price quote could be issued based upon moving 150 specified items with no packing services included. If however, on the day the mover arrives for the pick-up the consumer adds 30 additional boxes to be moved and also needs the movers to finish some of the packing the price will increase. Consumers hiring a regional independent moving company from a broker's network can save a great deal of money, but should have a very clear understanding of what services are and are not included in the price. Any extra service or additional items to be moved that were not included on the moving quote will increase the final price.

Option 3: Self pack and load - they drive container service.

Consumers wishing to do all the packing and loading themselves can hire a "container" service company. Generally, companies offering "container" services will drop off a large container at the home. It is up to the consumer to perform all the packing and loading of the container. Once they have completed the packing and loading the company will pick up the container and deliver it to the new home where the consumer will be responsible for unloading and unpacking.

Container services are good alternatives for people who do not need any assistance with packing or loading of their property. Container service companies charge based upon the size of the container rented, the distance the container is transported, and the number of days the container is used. Consumers need to be aware that container services may not offer insurance coverage for any damage or breakage of the property moved since it is self-packed. Additionally, container moving services for long distance interstate moves are not regulated by the government and therefore a consumer is not protected by the moving industry consumer protection laws.

Option 4: Complete do it yourself rent-a-truck moving.

Potentially, the least expensive option in moving is a full do it yourself move. Consumers choosing this option will borrow or rent a truck and do all the packing, loading, and driving themselves. Keeping in mind that moving is excruciatingly hard work, this is a good option if you have friends and family who can help and you don't mind taking on all the responsibility and stress for completing the move.

Costs associated with a self-service rent a truck move includes the costs of the rental truck, per mile charge, fuel charge, packing supplies, your time in driving, and in some cases pizza and drinks for your "volunteers."

Of the four options listed above the two with the biggest variations in pricing are the full service moves through a major van lines and the *á la carte* moving services offered from regional independent movers or movers in a broker's network.

How many people move per years in the United States?
According to the U.S. Census Bureau - 35.9 million U.S. residents, or 11.7 percent of all Americans, moved between 2012 and 2013.

This information comes from ***Geographical Mobility: 2012 to 2013***. The tables describe the movement of people in the United States, including type of move, reason for moving, distance moved and characteristics of those who moved one year earlier.

Hiring an Interstate Mover

CHAPTER 3

Hiring a professional moving company.

The long distance interstate moving industry is made up of professional, hard working, honest companies, estimators, drivers, and movers who provide reliable services. Most interstate long distance moves will be completed quickly and efficiently to the satisfaction of the consumer. However, as with any industry, there is always a chance of service failures, damaged or missing items, overcharges, and falling prey to unscrupulous and unlicensed individuals masquerading as licensed professional movers. The best way for a consumer shipper to prevent fraud, protect their property, and enforce their rights is to be an informed consumer who researches and hires a reputable professional moving company.

Long distance interstate moving involves moves that are picked up in one state and delivered into another state. A moving company is required to provide written estimates for their services. An estimate is not a bid or a contract and should not be considered as a guarantee of the price. Total actual charges for interstate moves are determined by the actual property "line-haul" (weight or cubic feet), packing labor and material, the number of miles traveled, and the extra services required to complete services (stairs, long carry, shuttle, storage, etc.).

This chapter is designed to help consumers research and hire a professional long distance interstate mover. Also included is information on how to plan a successful move as well as where and how to seek assistance in the event of problems.

Review the information in this chapter, do your homework before hiring a mover, and then you can benefit from services and experience of a reputable and reliable professional moving company. Always make certain to receive all estimates in writing and make sure all terms are clearly spelled out; never accept verbal promises or guarantees. Estimates must be complete, approved by the consumer, and signed BEFORE the moving company begins any work to pack or load the shipment.

Understanding the charges for moving services.

Generally, interstate moves performed by the nationally known major van lines or the regional independent moving companies are charged based on the weight of the property being transported or the amount of space (cubic feet) the property occupies on the truck, the distance traveled, time of year the move takes place, and the service options ordered.

If the charges are based upon weight a consumer should make certain to obtain a copy of the official certified scale certificates verifying the accuracy of the weight. After the goods have been packed and loaded the truck will be weighed to determine the "line-haul" charges. Only after the truck and property has been weighed and services performed can the actual final charges be determined.

Since the estimates are not typically guaranteed and the final price cannot be determined until services have been performed, the final actual charges could be higher or lower than the estimate. Generally, a consumer is only required to pay up to the amount of the last estimate issued to receive the property. Any charges above the last estimate issued are due thirty days after delivery.

It is standard practice for a moving company to offer extra services at an additional charge. An example of extra services not included in the weight or "line-haul" charges are for the use of expedited guaranteed delivery service, stairs, shuttle, long carry, elevator, packing and labor, storage, appliance services, etc. A consumer should have a clear understanding of what services are included in the estimate and what services will be charged at an additional rate

Possible reasons the final actual price may increase above the original interstate moving estimate.

Perhaps the biggest complaint consumers have about moving companies is that the final price of the move exceeded the original estimate. As previously explained charges for moving services are based on many factors which could be unknown before the services have been completed. In some cases it can be difficult to estimate the exact weight of all the property in a house, or if there will be special services required at the delivery destination.

A professional moving company should be able to give a reasonably accurate estimate. However, all estimates are based upon the information provided by the consumer. In some cases a consumer may not know if the extra services, such as stairs or long carry, will be required to complete delivery at the destination. There are many legitimate reasons the final changes for a move could end up higher than the original estimate given. Consumers need to be made aware in advance of the prices for extra services and be prepared to pay more money than originally anticipated if those services are required. Consider the following list of possible reasons the final cost of a move would increase above the estimate.

- After originally anticipating doing their own packing, the consumer runs out of time before the pick-up date and needs the mover to perform last minute packing services.

- A well intentioned conscientious consumer may request a moving estimate a month or two before their actual move date. Since the estimate was requested well in advance, the consumer did not have all their boxes packed when the estimator inquires "how many boxes will you be shipping?" It is difficult to accurately estimate the number of boxes which will be used to pack clothes, dishes, books, pantry items, garage items, and an entire household of miscellaneous items – when nothing has been packed.

• In the process of downsizing a customer may request an estimate based upon a specific list of items to be moved with the anticipation that they will sell, donate, or discard some of their current property. If the customer fails to sell, donate, or discard the property the size and cost of the move is increased.

• The estimator miscalculates the weight of certain items of furniture and ends up issuing an inaccurate estimate.

• Under the stress of planning a cross country move the consumer may simply forget to inform the estimator of seldom used items located in an attic, storage shed, or basement.

• In some cases a consumer may fail to inform the estimator of certain items to be moved in hope that they can lock in a lower price – not realizing that the final price would be based upon the weight of all the items moved (disclosed in advance or not) and services performed.

• The customer may not be familiar with the specific characteristics of the destination home resulting in extra unanticipated charges – i.e.

Shuttle charge: The use of a smaller truck to provide service to homes not accessible to the mover's normal 18 wheeler because of limited space or roadway restrictions. For example, delivery into downtown San Francisco.

Long Carry charge: A charge for carrying articles excessive distances between the mover's vehicle and the customer's home. For example, a 100 feet walkway from the street to the front door of the home.

Stairs: A charge for carrying items up or down flights of stairs. For example, delivery to the 5th floor of an apartment building with no functioning elevator.

Unanticipated storage: Temporary warehouse storage of the shipment pending further transportation. For example, if the consumer's new home isn't ready to occupy.

Rigging, hoisting, and lowering: Setting up a rope and pulley system to raise large bulky items through an upper floor window when the item will not fit though the front door. For example, an oversized couch, armoire or piano up to a second floor of an old Victorian home.

How to get an accurate estimate:

Accuracy of estimates are based in large part upon the accuracy of the information the consumer provides the estimator. Whether an estimate is given after an in-home visual inspection of the property or over the phone based upon a consumer's list of items to be moved – the accuracy depends on the information provided.

To help get an accurate estimate consumers need to fully inform the company of all items that will be moved and the specific services needed. A consumer should always obtain three written estimates to compare and check a mover's license and references. If you are going to use a professional moving company always make certain to hire a company that is properly licensed and insured. Consider the following list of tips to help ensure the accuracy of an estimate:

• Inform the estimator of all items being moved. Don't forget to list the items stored in an attic, storage unit, or garage.

• Describe in detail the physical location of the pick-up and delivery locations and inform the estimator if there will be stairs, excessively long walkways, or roadways inaccessible by a tractor trailer truck.

• Inform the estimator if you have any unusually large or bulky items being transported such as oversized pool tables, backyard playground sets, and/or large gym equipment.

• Let the estimator know if you need any special packing or wooden crating services of special items such as an antique vase or other large fragile items.

• Between the time you receive your initial estimate and the day of the move keep in contact with the estimator and provide updates if you decide to move additional items, change the services ordered, or need the movers to pack your property. Informing the estimator of changes or updates to your move before the day of the pick-up will the let you see an updated estimate so you can avoid surprise price increases.

• Let the estimator know if you need to order expedited or guaranteed delivery service or if you want the less expensive standard non-guaranteed ground transport service.

Protecting your property: Insurance vs. Valuation

Insurance is an agreement by which one party assumes a risk faced by another party in return for a premium payment. Valuation is not insurance. Valuation is the degree of worth of the shipment. The valuation charge compensates the mover for assuming a greater degree of liability than is provided for in its base transportation charges. In practical application, valuation is the agreement between the parties as to a moving company's limitation of liability in the event of any loss or damage.

The basic free level of valuation coverage is the standard basic liability option of $0.60 cents per pound per article. Insurance coverage is not automatically included in your moving contract. If you wish to have full replacement value protection, you should consider purchasing full coverage insurance. The moving company estimator should be able to provide you a quote for full insurance coverage or direct you to a third party moving insurance company. (For more information see chapter 12).

Example: Under the Limited Liability valuation option a moving company will only be liable for up to $0.60 per pound per article for any items damaged or lost during an interstate move. For example, if a 10 pound laptop computer valued at $2,000 is lost or destroyed the consumer shipper would only receive $6.00 in compensation ($0.60 x 10 pounds = $6.00).

Understanding delivery windows.

Transporting an entire household of property long distances is a complex logistical task. In most cases, specific delivery dates are not guaranteed. Long distance interstate moving takes time. You should have a clear understanding and written confirmation of the pickup and delivery windows. In many cases, the delivery windows could be up to 10, 15 or even 30 days or longer. If you need your property by a certain date, then you must receive written confirmation of the delivery dates or window in writing from the moving company before you hire them. ***A mover should not give and a consumer should not accept verbal promises of delivery dates; all estimates must be confirmed in writing.***

Understanding shipment consolidation.

A consumer should be made aware that, unless otherwise stated in writing, the property could be consolidated with other customer property on the same truck while transported. Also, oftentimes the property will not stay on the same truck that performed the pickup. To help organize and consolidate shipments it is not unusual that the property will be offloaded, temporarily stored, and then transported on different trucks or by subcontractors. These issues should be clarified with the moving company before the consumer and the mover enter into a moving contract for services.

> **Consumer tip:** If a consumer does not wish to have their property consolidated and transported with property belonging to other consumer shippers, then a consumer should specify that their order include "exclusive use of the vehicle" service to ensure that the property will not be consolidated and they will have the exclusive use of the truck.

What if there is a problem?

Most moves are picked up and delivered problem free. However, when there is a problem with a shipment a consumer has several options to have the issues resolved. Problems with a shipment can range from delivery delays, or damages and missing items, or unexpected storage needs, to disputes over charges. Whatever the issues, the moving company should work with the consumer to help answer any questions and to resolve any concerns. Consider the following options in attempting to express your concerns to the moving company and having the issues resolved.

Customer service department. A professional moving company should have a dedicated customer service department that can answer any questions concerning your move and work with you to resolve any issues. During the transportation of your shipment you should stay in contact with the moving company customer service department. Advise the company if you need to make any changes to your order, have a special request, or have problems with your shipment. If a problem arises during the transportation, delivery, or after delivery call the customer service department and give them an opportunity to answer your questions and resolve your concerns.

Filing a claim for damages or missing items. All customers have an absolute right to file a claim for damaged or missing items. If your goods are damaged or missing at delivery ask the moving company to send you a claim form so you can list your damages. Once the claim form is received, the moving company must process your claim and offer you repairs or compensation in accordance with the valuation or insurance option you selected. You must file a written claim with the mover within 9 months of delivery. Your claim must be in writing but does not have to be submitted on a mover's claim form. If you receive the settlement offer from the moving company and are not satisfied you are not required to accept the offer. If you do not agree with the claim settlement offer, you have the option of submitting a claim with the mover's neutral dispute settlement program or to seek other legal remedies.

Neutral dispute settlement program. A moving company must offer their customers a neutral dispute settlement program as a means of settling disputes that may arise concerning loss, damage, or overcharges resulting from the transportation of your household goods. A neutral dispute settlement program (or arbitration program) is available at the option of the customer. A moving company may not require that you use the arbitration program. If your claim is $10,000 or less then the moving company is required to submit to binding arbitration if you choose arbitration. If your claim is $10,000 or more, then you may request arbitration, but the moving company may decline submitting to arbitration. Arbitration is typically not free. You and the moving company may be required to split the costs for the arbitration services 50/50. Arbitration is an alternative to courtroom litigation and may be a method to resolve disputes faster, less expensively, and more efficiently than traditional courtroom litigation.

Consumer Protection tip. Where to file a complaint against an interstate moving company. The United States Department of Transportation Federal Motor Carrier Safety Administration (FMCSA) licenses and regulates interstate moving companies. You may file a complaint against a moving company by visiting http://nccdb.fmcsa.dot.gov or calling 1-888-DOT-SAFT (1-888-368-7238) Monday–Friday, between the hours of 9:00 a.m. to 9:00 p.m. EST.

Filing a lawsuit against a mover. As a consumer, you always have the legal right to file a lawsuit against your moving company if you feel you have a case. Depending on the allegations in your lawsuit you may choose to file in small claims court or district court. You should review the moving company contract terms and conditions to determine if there is a valid jurisdiction provision that requires you to file your lawsuit in the state and county where the company is headquartered. Decisions over what type of lawsuit to file, what allegations to make, and where to file should be considered carefully. When considering courtroom litigation it is advised that you hire an attorney to evaluate your case, give you legal advice, and explain your legal options.

Interstate Moving Q&A

CHAPTER 4

The following section contains answers to many common questions a consumer should ask when considering which moving company to hire. Each moving company may create prices, payment terms, and company policies that may differ from other moving companies. It is important to research several moving companies and compare the service options they provide, the price for their services, and their performance records. When a consumer hires a moving company they are entrusting all of their worldly possessions to the mover's care. It is important that they make their selection of a moving company based upon careful research and not price alone.

1. Are interstate moving companies required to be licensed?

2. How do I check if the moving company is licensed?

3. Can the company be penalized for operating without a license?

4. Is a deposit required to book a move?

5. Are written estimates required?

6. Must the moving company offer me an in-home estimates?

7. Is an estimate a guarantee of the price?

8. What types of estimates are given?

9. Can the price on a "binding" estimate be changed or increased?

10. Should I read the estimate and contracts before signing?

11. How does a mover calculate the total charges for my move?

12. Will I be asked to sign blank or incomplete documents?

13. Must I be present on the day of the pick up?

14. Can I pay for the move with a credit card?

15. Is a moving company required to weigh my property?

16. How long will a moving company take to deliver my property?

17. Can I cancel my move after I receive an estimate?

18. Will my property be the only property on the truck?

19. Must a moving company have a neutral arbitration program?

20. Can the moving company use subcontractors?

21. Will a moving company charge extra for packing materials?

22. Will insurance automatically cover my property against damages?

23. How long do I have to file a claim for damages or missing items?

24. Can I sue my moving company if my property was damaged?

25. Can I cancel my move after the goods have been picked up?

26. What do I do if the movers are holding my property hostage?

27. Will movers charge more depending on the time of year I move?

28. What items am I not allowed to move?

29. Can I move part of my property to my home and part into storage?

30. Will the movers disassemble and reassemble my furniture?

31. Can I inspect my property for damages before I pay the final bill?

32. What if I can't afford to pay the final bill in full at the delivery?

33. Will my homeowners insurance cover my property while it is being transported by the moving company?

1. Are interstate moving companies required to be licensed?

Yes, all interstate moving companies are required to have a license issued by the United States Department of Transportation FMCSA. A properly licensed moving company will have a "MC" (Motor Carrier) number and US DOT license number. A consumer should never hire the services or trust their personal property to an unlicensed company.

2. How do I check if the moving company is licensed?

You can check the license and authority status of any moving company by searching the US DOT website:
http://safer.fmcsa.dot.gov/CompanySnapshot.aspx

3. Can the company be penalized for operating without a license?

A company who performs interstate moving services without being properly licensed can receive a fine from the US DOT in the amount of $25,000.

4. Is a deposit required to book a move?

Each individual moving company is allowed to set their own rules for deposits and terms of payment. Terms of payment and deposits must be disclosed to each customer in writing. It is not uncommon for a moving company to request a small booking deposit to secure the space on the truck. When comparing the services of moving companies a customer should also compare the deposit and payment policies before making a selection of a mover.

5. Are written estimates required?

Yes, a moving company must issue a written estimate of the proposed services for an interstate move. The estimate must list all services being offered and the estimated charges for the completed move. A customer should not accept verbal estimates or promises. All estimates must be in writing. See chapter 5 for more information.

6. Must the moving company offer me an in-home estimate?

A moving company must provide an estimate based upon an in-home visual inspection of the property if the pick-up location is located within fifty miles of the moving company headquarters. The choice to have an in-home estimate or not is the customers. If a customer does not wish to have an in-home estimate they may waive that right. See chapter 5 for more information. See 49 USC Section 14104(b)(1)(C).

7. Is an estimate a guarantee of the price?

Estimates are not guarantees of the total charges. An estimate is an approximation of the total final charges based upon a specific set of services ordered and items to be moved. A customer should be advised that if additional services are ordered, required to be performed, or additional items (weight or cubic feet) are shipped then the price may increase.

8. What types of estimates are given?

Moving companies are required to issue written estimates as either "binding" or "non-binding." The law governing moving companies does not have a provision for any type of estimate other than "binding" or "non-binding." For example, estimates issued as "not to exceed" or "guaranteed not to exceed" or "flat rate price" are not specifically allowed under any provision of federal law.

9. Can the price on a "binding" estimate be changed or increased?

Yes. A binding estimate is not a bid or a contract. The term "binding" can be misleading in that it is only binding for the specific goods and services itemized in writing. If a customer moves more items or request additional services the final price will increase, despite the fact that the estimate was "binding." Read all estimates carefully and completely before signing.

10. Should I read the estimate and contracts before signing?

Yes. A customer should always read all the terms and conditions of a moving company estimate and contract for services before signing. Estimates and contracts contain very important legal terms that will affect how much you pay for services, when the goods are to be delivered, and what protections you will have against damaged or missing items. All documents should be carefully read and understood before a customer signs anything.

11. How does a moving company calculate the total charges for my move?

Most charges for interstate moves are calculated based on the weight of the property being transported or the amount of space (cubic feet) the property occupies on the truck. If the charges are based upon weight, after the goods have been packed and loaded, the truck will be weighed to determine the line-haul charges. Only after the truck and property has been weighed can the charges be determined. Since estimates are not guaranteed, the final charges could be higher or lower than the estimate. It is standard practice for a moving company to offer extra services at an additional charge. Examples of extra services include the use of stairs, shuttle, long carry, elevator, packing and labor, storage, appliance services, etc. See chapter 11 for more information.

12. Will I be asked to sign blank or incomplete documents?

Consumers should ***never*** sign blank documents. However, in some cases it is acceptable to sign incomplete documents. Since the final charges for the moving services cannot be determined until after the goods have been loaded and weighed (when based upon weight) some of the documents a consumer shipper is required to sign at the time of pick-up will be incomplete and not contain the final charges. Signing a bill of lading at the pick-up that is incomplete and does not contain the final charges is not illegal or unusual since final charges are not known at the time of pick-up. However, the estimate or revised written estimate must ***never*** be signed blank or incomplete. At the time the estimate or revised written estimate is signed it must contain an itemization of all services and the total estimated charges. A consumer shipper should never sign an estimate or revised written estimate that does not list the total estimated charges. See 49 CFR Section 375.501(d).

13. Must I be present on the day of the pick up?

Yes. On the date of pick-up several important shipping documents must be signed by the customer. It is also very important that the customer supervise the work and make certain the mover is performing as agreed. If it is impossible for the customer to be present on the day of the pick-up they can designate, in writing, an agent/representative to act on their behalf and sign the contract. A customer should think very carefully before granting permission to an agent/representative. The customer will be legally bound by the choices made, acts, and signatures of their agent/representative.

14. Can I pay for the move with a credit card?

Each individual moving company is allowed to set their own rules and policies concerning the acceptance of credit cards and other terms of payment. Terms of payment must be disclosed to each customer in writing. Moving companies can set policies accepting credit cards for the entire move or just the deposit. When comparing the services of moving companies a customer should also compare the forms of payment policies before making a selection of a mover.

15. Is a moving company required to weigh my property?

If the charges for services are based upon the weight of the property, then yes. When the moving company provides services based upon a non-binding estimate to be charged by weight they must determine the weight of each shipment. Alternatively, if the charges are to be determined based upon an hourly rate or by a "binding cubic feet" rate then the law does not require the moving company to obtain weight certificates.

16. How long will a moving company take to deliver my property?

In most cases specific delivery dates are not guaranteed. Delivery windows could be up to 10, 15 or even 30 days or longer. Customers must have a clear understanding and written confirmation of the pick-up and delivery windows before hiring a moving company. If you need your property by a certain date, then you must receive written confirmation of the delivery dates or window from the moving company before you hire them. Do not accept verbal promises of delivery dates. You must receive confirmation of delivery dates in writing.

17. Can I cancel my move after I receive an estimate?

Yes. An estimate is not a bid or a contract and may be canceled anytime before the move begins. Either the customer or the moving company may cancel the estimate before services begin and before the bill of lading (contract) is signed. For example, if on the day of the move the moving company increases the estimated price to an amount the customer does not agree with; the customer may cancel the services. Once services begin and the bill of lading is signed neither the moving company nor the customer can cancel the move.

18. Will my property be the only property on the truck?

Often times the property will not stay on the same truck that performed the pick-up. To help organize and consolidate shipments it is not unusual that the property will be offloaded, temporarily stored, and then transported on different trucks or by subcontractors. Unless otherwise stated in writing, a customer's property could be consolidated with other customer property on the same truck while being transported. These issues should be clarified with the moving company before you sign a contract for services.

19. Must a moving company have a neutral arbitration program?

Yes. A moving company must offer their customers a neutral dispute settlement program as a means of settling disputes that may arise concerning loss, damage, or overcharges resulting from the transportation the property. Arbitration is an alternative to courtroom litigation and may be a method to resolve disputes faster, less expense, and more efficiently than traditional courtroom litigation. Arbitration is typically not free. You and the moving company may be required to split the costs for the arbitration services 50/50. See chapter 15 for more information.

20. Can the moving company use subcontractors?

Yes. It is not uncommon for a moving company to use a subcontractor to perform all or a portion of the moving services. The primary moving company who booked the job may legally subcontract out the job to another properly licensed moving company to perform part or all of the services. Even if they use a subcontractor, the primary moving company will ultimately be responsible for the actions or omissions of the subcontractors. You should ask a moving company if they will use subcontractors before you sign a contract for services. See 49 CFR Section 375.205.

21. Will a moving company charge extra for packing materials?

Typically packing labor and materials are not included in the base line-haul and will be charged as an extra service. Packing labor and materials may be available at a fixed fee per item/box or on an hourly basis. Customers should be aware that many moving companies charge a premium for packing materials. If you are going to have the movers pack your property you should make certain to receive and compare the mover's packing materials price list before you select a moving company.

22. Will insurance automatically cover my property against damages?

Moving companies are required to maintain cargo and liability insurance as part of their license. However, many cargo policies do not fully cover a customer's property. Insurance coverage should not be assumed to be automatically included in the price of the move.

Customers wishing to have full coverage insurance should ask the estimator about insurance coverage options and independently purchase third party insurance coverage. See chapter 12 for more information.

23. How long do I have to file a claim for damages or missing items?

If any items of property are damaged or missing the customer has a right to file a claim for compensation. Compensation for the damaged or missing property will be based upon the coverage level selected by the customer. Full value coverage is not automatic. A customer has nine months from the date of delivery to file their claim for damaged or missing property. See chapter 14 for more information.

24. Can I sue my moving company if my property was damaged?

A customer always has the legal right to file a lawsuit against the moving company if they have been damaged. Decisions over what type of lawsuit to file, what allegations to make, and where to file should be considered carefully. When considering courtroom litigation it is advised that customers hire an attorney to evaluate the case, give professional legal advice, and explain the various legal options.

25. Can I cancel my move after the goods have been picked up?

After the bill of lading (contract) has been signed and the services have begun neither the customer nor the moving company can cancel the contract without the consent of the other. For example, after the pick-up when you are waiting for your property to be delivered, the moving company can't call and tell you that they have decided not to complete your move. Even if they offer to give you your money back, the moving company can't simply cancel the move after services have begun. Similarly, a customer may not cancel the services of the moving company after the move has begun. Canceling the move after services have begun would be a breach of contract and actionable in court. In reality, people cancel moves all the time. Many times and for many reasons customers or moving companies need to cancel the moving services. In such cases, the move can only be canceled if the customer and the moving company both agree on when to cancel, how to cancel, and what payment is owed for the services already performed. Cancelations after the pick-up can only occur if both the moving company and the customer agree.

26. What do I do if the movers are holding my property hostage?

The maximum amount of money a moving company can collect at the delivery (prior to unloading) is the total amount of the estimate (or total amount of the revised estimate), plus additional services performed as post contract services, plus 10% if a non-binding estimate. Any remaining balance due must be billed after 30 days of delivery. If a moving company refuses to deliver the property unless you pay an amount of money greater than the estimate (or revised written estimate), plus the post contract services performed, plus 10% if a non-binding estimate, then the moving company would be acting illegally and holding the goods hostage. Moving companies demanding more money than the total amount of the estimate (or revised written estimate) plus post contract services performed should be immediately reported to the US DOT. If the US DOT investigates the matter and finds that the moving company has acted illegally, the moving company could face civil and criminal charges.

27. Will movers charge more depending on the time of year I move?

Yes. Moving is a seasonal business and charges for moving services may differ depending on the time of year you are moving. Generally, peak season takes place in the summer. During the peak season moves will be charged at premium rates. Moves taking place in the winter may be charged at a lower rate than a similar move in the summer. Rates for services, accessorial charges, and labor charges will differ from company to company and should be compared before selecting a moving company.

28. What items am I not allowed to move?

In a normal interstate move, customers may not ship and moving companies may not transport items which are perishable, dangerous, or hazardous materials. A customer who packs such items without the moving company's knowledge may be subject to civil and criminal penalties. (49 USC section 5124).

29. Can I move part of my property to my home and part into storage?

Multiple pick-ups or deliveries in a single move are not unusual. At times a customer may need the majority of their property delivered to their new home and a portion of their property delivered into a storage unit. Deliveries to multiple locations for the same move are known as split deliveries. Most moving companies will offer a split pick-up or delivery service at an extra service charge.

30. Will the movers disassemble and reassemble my furniture?

Services offered by a moving company will differ from company to company. Disassembly and reassembly of furniture or appliances is a service that not all moving companies may offer. Full service moving companies offering a disassembly and reassembly service may do so at an extra service fee. It is important to discuss special services such as furniture assembly and disassembly with the estimator before selecting a moving company.

31. Can I inspect my property for damages before I pay the final bill?

Moving services may be performed under payment terms allowing for billing after delivery or under COD terms. If your moving services were performed under delayed billing terms then you will receive your property, have the opportunity to inspect your goods, and then pay for the services after you have been billed. However, if your moving services are to be performed under COD terms then full payment must be made prior to you having the opportunity to inspect your property. COD shipments are generally paid in full prior to the truck being unloaded. Each moving company may have different policies for payment. It is important to have a clear understanding of the form and timeline for payment before selecting a moving company.

32. What if I can't afford to pay the final bill in full at the delivery?

If the final legitimate bill for services is higher than the customer can afford to pay, a moving company generally has two options. First, the moving company at their discretion may extend credit to the customer by delivering the property and billing the balance at a later time. Alternatively, the moving company may exercise their carrier's lien by refusing to deliver and placing the property into storage until the bill is paid. If a customer's property has been placed into storage the final bill will be increased to cover the cost of storage and re-delivery. If the legitimate bill remains unpaid the moving company may eventually sell the property at public auction.

33. Will my homeowner insurance cover my property while it is being transported by the moving company?

In some cases a customer's homeowner insurance policy will cover damage to consumer goods while the goods are being transported by the moving company. Coverage is not automatic. A customer should check directly with their own homeowner insurance company to determine if coverage is available.

Estimates

CHAPTER 5

Are written estimates required for each move?

Yes. A moving company must provide a written estimate to each prospective consumer shipper. An estimate must list all charges for transportation, accessorial services, advance charges, and the form of payment accepted. Both the consumer shipper and a representative from the moving company must sign and date each estimate. (49 CFR Section 375.401(a)).

Is the estimate a contract?

No. An estimate is neither a bid nor a contract. It is merely an approximation of what the move may cost based on the services listed on the estimate. The only contract between a moving company and a consumer shipper is the "bill of lading." The moving company or the consumer shipper may cancel the move at anytime prior to a bill of lading being signed. Consumer shippers should be aware that the charges listed on the estimate are not guaranteed and that the actual charges of the move may be higher or lower than the amount estimated.

Are visual in-home estimates required?

Generally, yes. Under US DOT regulations, consumer shippers with property located within 50 miles of the estimator's location must receive a physical survey/visual estimate of the property. The estimate must be prepared in writing, signed by both the consumer shipper and moving company, and state whether it is binding or non-binding. Federal law under 49 USC Section 14104(b)(1)(C) requires that estimates (both binding and non-binding) be in writing and be based on a visual in-home inspection of the property if the consumer shipper's pickup location is within a 50 mile radius of the location of the moving company's household goods agent preparing the estimate.

Waiver exception: a visual estimate is NOT required if (1) the pickup address is outside the 50 mile radius or (2) a written waiver is signed by the consumer shipper stating that they waive their right to a visual in-home estimate. (49 USC 14104(b)(1)(B).)

> Prior to the move actually starting, either the moving company or the consumer shipper may cancel move. However, after the move has begun, neither party may unilaterally cancel the contract for services without penalty.

What types of estimates are allowed?

Federal law governing interstate moving companies requires that the consumer shipper receive a written and reasonably accurate estimate of all charges for the services proposed. Federal law permits and requires only two types of estimates: BINDING and NON-BINDING. The written estimate document must expressly state whether it is BINDING or NON-BINDING and must be signed by both the moving company and the consumer shipper. (49 CFR section 375.401(a)).

Federal law does not have a provision for any type of estimate other than BINDING or NON-BINDING. For example, estimates issued as "not to exceed" or "guaranteed not to exceed" or "flat rate price" are not specifically allowed under any provision of federal law.

Non-binding estimate.

A non-binding estimate is the estimated total cost of the entire move, based upon the estimated weight of the shipment and the accessorial services requested. A non-binding estimate is meant to give the consumer shipper a general idea of the cost of the move. The non-binding estimate is not a guarantee that the actual charges will not be higher than estimated. The estimate document must explain to the customer in easy to understand language that the final charges are based on the actual weight of the property and accessorial services.

Non-binding estimates must be in writing and clearly describe the shipment and all services proposed. (49 CFR section 375.405(b)(6)). Any time a moving company provides such an estimate, the amount of the charges estimated must be transferred to the order for service and/or bill of lading. The figures on both documents must match. Non-binding estimates must be provided to a prospective consumer shipper for free. (49 CFR section 375.405(b)(3)).

Consumer protection tip. Always make certain to receive all estimates in writing and make sure all terms are clearly spelled out; never accept verbal promises or guarantees. Estimates must be completed, approved by the customer, and signed BEFORE the moving company begins any work to pack or load the shipment.

The 110% Rule only applies to non-binding estimates. Under the 110% Rule, the moving company may only demand the total charges listed on the estimate (or revised written estimate) plus 10%. If the consumer shipper pays the amount of the estimate plus 10%, then the moving company must deliver all of the consumer shipper's property even if the consumer shipper stills owes a balance.[1] See chapter 7 for more information)

When a move is to be charged based on weight, the final charges will be determined by the actual weight of the shipment, the services provided, and its tariff provisions in effect. A consumer shipper should be prepared to pay up to 10% more than the estimated amount at delivery. The final charges for a move will be based upon and in accordance with the moving company's published tariff.

If the consumer shipper orders additional services after the goods are in transit, the moving company will then bill the shipper 30 days after delivery for any remaining charges. (49 CFR section 375.405(b)(10)). However, if the moving company believes that additional services are needed after the goods are in transit, the company must first inform the consumer shipper of the additional service and obtain their approval. (49 CFR section 375.405(b)(9)).

---

[1] *NOTE: The 110% Rule does not apply to post contract services. A moving company may collect advance charges for post contract services.*

	The following information must be included in an interstate moving company estimate and provided to consumers:
☐	A concise, easy-to-read, accurate estimate of the moving company's charges including all accessorial charges.
☐	A clear statement specifying if the estimate is "Binding" or "Non-Binding"
☐	A clear statement specifying the form of payment accepted.
☐	The estimate must be signed by both the consumer shipper and moving company representative.
☐	A consumer must be provided a copy of the booklet entitled, "Your Rights and Responsibilities When You Move."
☐	The estimate must contain a notice of the availability of the moving company's tariff for the estimate of charges, including an explanation that individual shippers are entitled to copies.
☐	The estimate must include a concise, easy-to-read, accurate summary of the moving company's arbitration program.
☐	The estimate must include a concise, easy to read, accurate summary of the moving company's customer complaint and inquiry handling procedures.
☐	The consumer must be provided with a copy of the pamphlet entitled "Ready to Move." (49 USC 14104(b)(2).
☐	The estimate must include both valuation options as mandated by the Surface Transportation Board's release rates order.

The myth of "binding" estimates.

A binding estimate is an agreement made in advance between the consumer shipper and the moving company. It provides that the total cost of the move will be based upon the description of services and quantity of items (item list) shown on the binding estimate. (49 CFR section 375.401(a)(1)).

The term "binding" is misleading in that it suggests that the total amount listed on the binding estimate is guaranteed. This is not the case. A binding estimate may be "revised" on the date of pickup, prior to any work beginning, for a higher charge based on additional services or items being transported.

A binding estimate must be in writing, state that it is "binding", and contain the signatures of both the moving company and the consumer shipper. A binding estimate must clearly describe the shipment and all services provided. (49 CFR section 375.403(a)(4)). A moving company may charge a consumer shipper a fee for providing a binding estimate. (49 USC 14104(b)(1)(C)(ii)).

Generally, when charges are based on binding estimates the consumer shipper will not be required to pay more than the estimated amount at delivery. The charges are due at the time of delivery, prior to unloading in compliance with the moving company's published tariff. (49 CFR section 375.407(a)).

If the consumer shipper has requested additional or accessorial services that were not listed on the estimate, the moving company may demand full payment for those added post contract services at the time of delivery prior to unloading. Such services might include destination charges that often are not known at origin (such as long carry charges, shuttle charges, or extra stair carry charges). See chapter 11 for more information.

Consumer tip. A binding estimate is not a bid or a contract. The term "binding" can be misleading in that it is only binding for the specific goods and services itemized in writing. If you move more items or request additional services the final price will increase, despite the fact that the estimate was "binding." Read all estimates carefully and completely before signing.

Revised written estimate or rescission.

An estimate, whether binding or non-binding, may be increased or decreased in price any time prior to the work beginning. In accordance with 49 CFR § 305.403(a)(6)(ii) and/or 49 CFR § 305.405(b)(7)(ii): If prior to or on the day of the scheduled pickup the consumer shipper tenders more property or makes a change to the initial order for which they received an estimate the moving company may either:

(1) undertake the job with the additional property in which case the consumer shipper would only be required to pay 10% more than the initial estimate to receive the property on a non-binding estimate or 100% of the binding estimate with the remaining balance to be billed after the 30 day deferment; ***or***

(2) the moving company and consumer shipper may execute a revised written estimate/rescission document **PRIOR TO LOADING OR OTHERWISE BEGINNING THE JOB**.

The revised written estimate given prior to loading will serve as the only active estimate for which charges will be calculated. In effect, the Revised Written Estimate cancels the original estimate and acts as the new governing estimate. To change an estimate, the consumer shipper and the moving company must both agree to make changes and must do so before the shipment has been loaded. (49 CFR section 375.401(g)).

For example, a consumer shipper may receive over the telephone a binding estimate based on 200 items to be moved for a price of $2,000. Based upon that estimate, the consumer shipper will book the move, pay the deposit, make travel arrangements, and plan to vacate their home on the scheduled moving date. However, when the moving company arrives on the pickup date, they visually inspect the property and determines, prior to beginning any work, that there will be 400 items to be moved and not the originally estimated 200 items. This situation creates problems for both the moving company and the consumer shipper.

Confronted with the situation described above, a moving company may rescind/cancel the original estimate (binding or non-binding) and provide the consumer shipper with two options. First, cancel the job in its entirety; or second, create a revised written estimate based upon 400 items to be moved at a price of $4,000. If the customer agrees to the new price and signs the revised written estimate, then the original estimate is canceled and the goods will be transported under the terms and price of the new estimate.

This situation is not a good option for either the moving company or the consumer shipper. Consumer shippers may feel like they have no choice but to agree to the new price because they have made plans scheduled around the move date. Nevertheless, in this situation, assuming the revised estimate was written and signed correctly and provided in good faith to the consumer shipper before the moving services began, the moving company has acted appropriately.

A last minute addition in the property a consumer is transporting, or services they are ordering, creates logistical problems and increases expenses of the moving company. To maintain profitability moving companies follow a structured logistical planed route for each truck which is based upon space allocation for each customer. A moving company tractor trailer transports multiple consumer households at one time (shipment consolidation). If a consumer shipper decided at the last minute to move more items; the next customer on the pick-up schedule will not have room for their property which causes delays, complaints, and increased cost to the company.

Most moving companies would agree that last minute changes to a consumer's shipment can result in additional expenses to the company and logistical nightmares associated with the unexpected changes. As such, providing accurate, honest estimates to consumers is a critical necessity. Both consumers and moving companies must take proactive steps to avoid this situation.

How consumer shippers can protect their property and prevent unexpected charges:
1. Do your homework before hiring a mover. Check references, make certain the mover is properly licensed, and understand the terms of the estimate provided.
2. Make certain to provide the estimator an accurate listing of the items to be moved.
3. If, after receiving the original estimate, you have added items to be moved or require additional services, inform the estimator so the original estimate can be updated.
4. Ask the mover for a copy of the price list for accessorial or extra charges such as stairs, long carry, shuttle, packing, appliance servicing, fuel surcharges, or origin/destination fees.
5. Make certain all estimates are in writing and properly itemize the services and charges for each. NOTE: if added services are required to complete the move, then you will be charged an additional fee.

Safeguard against low-ball estimates

CHAPTER 6

How to prevent "low-balling" and abuse of revised written estimates.

Low-balling an estimate is a serious crime. Interstate brokers and moving companies have a responsibility to protect their customers against this type of criminal fraud. As part of this responsibility management should set company-wide standards to ensure the accuracy of estimates, and monitor estimators to safeguard against "low-balling."

The revised written estimate is a tool authorized by FMCSA regulation to be used in situations where the consumer shipper has made last minute additions to the property being transported or if they order last minute services – such as packing or storage. 49 CFR § 305.403(a)(6)(ii) and/or 49 CFR § 305.405(b)(7)(ii). The revised written estimate cancels the original estimate and creates a new higher estimate accounting for the additional property to be transported or services ordered by the consumer shipper.

A revised written estimate which has been reviewed, authorized, and signed by the consumer shipper prior to the start of moving services will serve as the only active estimate for which charges will be calculated. In effect, the revised written estimate cancels the original estimate and acts as the new governing estimate.

A revised written estimate is an important and legitimate tool to be used when the consumer shipper makes an unplanned last minute addition to the services ordered. However, some dishonest motor carriers have abused this process by purposefully "low-balling" the original estimate in anticipation of using a revised written estimate to increase the charges for services at the last minute.

WARNING: Low-balling estimates is a crime. Companies must take steps to safeguard against low-ball estimates. There are many situations where the legitimate use of a revised written estimate is necessary. However, **company management should have safeguards in place to prevent "low-balling."** A simple step management can take is to calculate the percentage of total jobs where a revised written estimate was used to increase the estimate on the day of the move. For example, if 90% of a particular estimator's booked moves increased on the day of the move – then there is a problem with the quality of original estimates being issued. If original estimates are honest and accurate then the percentage of estimate increases on the day of the move should be relatively low.

When confronted with the fraudulent use of a revised written estimate, consumer shippers may have little choice but to agree to the inflated price because they are forced into a position where they cannot reasonably find another moving company at the last minute. The consumer would have presumably made travel arrangements, or gave notice to vacate their home, or scheduled the start of a new job, etc. -- in good faith reliance on the accuracy of the original estimate. An interstate broker or moving company "low-balling" and purposefully abusing a revised written estimate in this manner is guilty of criminal fraud and extortion.[2]

Interstate moving companies have a responsibility to protect their customers against this type of fraud. As part of this responsibility management should set company-wide standards to ensure the accuracy of estimates, and monitor estimators to safeguard against "low-balling." To help safeguard against "low-balling" and revised written estimate abuse interstate movers could do the following:

---

[2] See 18 USC §§ 371; 1343; 1951; 1956(h); 1956(a)(1(A)(1)

Safeguard against "low-balling" and abuse of a revised written estimate by:

1. Provide consumer shippers with honest estimates based on a detailed and an accurate item list and services to be performed.

2. Prior to the moving day inform the consumer shipper of the possibility and rates for all additional charges and optional services.

3. Prior to the moving day make certain the consumer shipper understands that the price is not guaranteed if additional items are moved or additional services ordered.

4. Verify the accuracy of the original estimate by contacting the consumer shipper several days prior to the move to confirm the services ordered and find out if any changes have been made to the number of items to be moved or services requested and inform the consumer of any changes to the price.

5. Regularly monitor the percentage of total moves where the original estimate increased on the day of the move. If original estimates are honest and accurate then the percentage of estimate increases on the day of the move should be relatively low.

6. Establish a company-wide policy that prevents interline agent carriers to issue a revised written estimate without prior company authorization. By requiring company authorization, management can confirm with the customer that the need for a revised written estimate is legitimate, in compliance with the governing regulations, and that it was approved it in good faith prior to servicing beginning.

7. If there is a legitimate reason to revise an estimate, make certain to use a revised written estimate form that contains a warning to the consumer shipper not to sign blank documents.

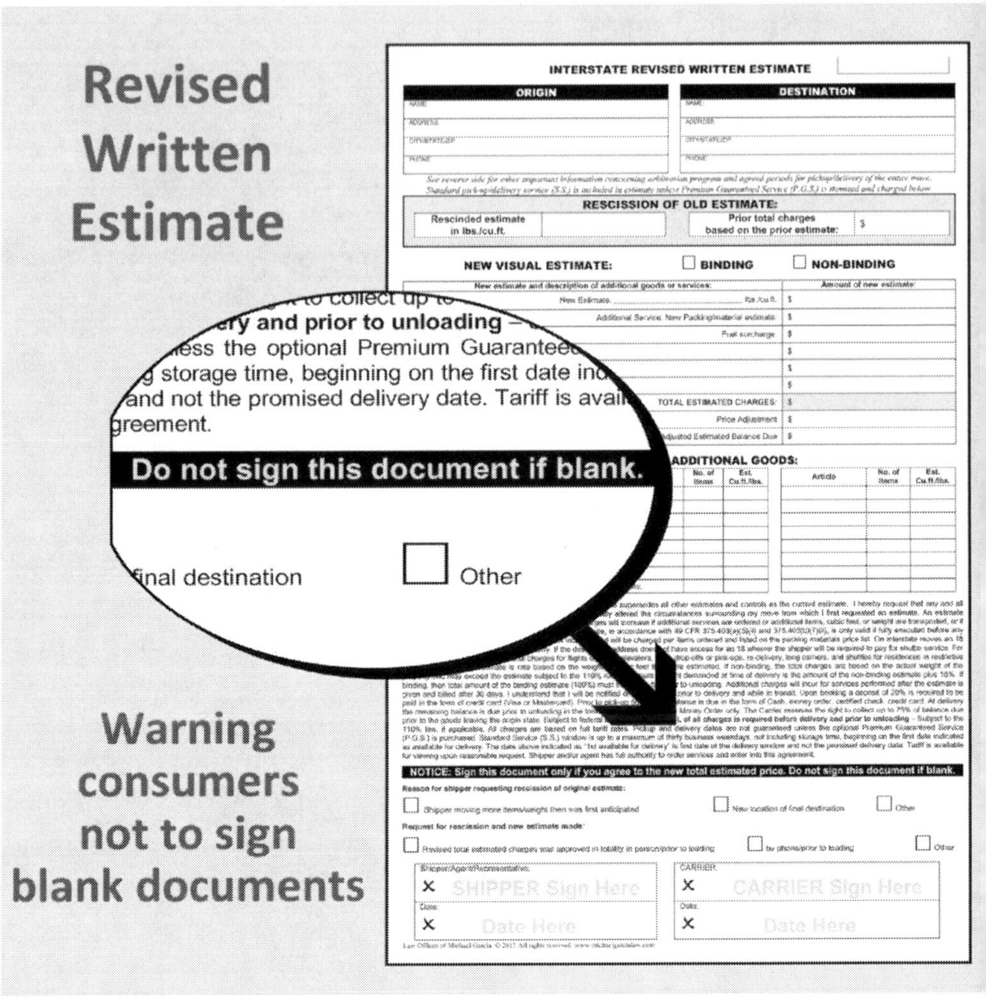
Revised Written Estimate
Warning consumers not to sign blank documents
INTERSTATE REVISED WRITTEN ESTIMATE
ORIGIN
DESTINATION
RESCISSION OF OLD ESTIMATE:
Rescinded estimate in lbs./cu.ft.
Prior total charges based on the prior estimate:
NEW VISUAL ESTIMATE:
BINDING
NON-BINDING
ery and prior to unloading
ess the optional Premium Guarantee
storage time, beginning on the first date ind
and not the promised delivery date. Tariff is avai
greement.
Do not sign this document if blank.
final destination
Other
TOTAL ESTIMATED CHARGES:
ADDITIONAL GOODS:
NOTICE: Sign this document only if you agree to the new total estimated price. Do not sign this document if blank.
SHIPPER Sign Here
CARRIER Sign Here
Date Here
Date Here

The 110% Rule

CHAPTER 7

The 110% Rule is an important consumer protection law controlling the delivery of interstate household goods based on ***non-binding*** written estimates. The 110% Rule applies in situations when the total final charges of the move have exceeded the controlling written non-binding estimate by more than 10%. Under those circumstances the rule requires that the moving company deliver all of the consumer shipper's property if the consumer shipper pays 100% of the amount listed on the controlling written non-binding estimate plus an additional 10%. (49 CFR section 375.407).

For example, if the controlling written non-binding estimate for services was $2,000 and the total final charges, based upon the actual weight of the property is $3,000 then under this rule the moving company must deliver all of the property if the consumer shipper pays $2,200. The remaining $800 balance will be billed to the consumer shipper and is due 30 days after delivery.

Does the 110% Rule apply to a binding estimate?

No. The 110% Rule allows a shipper to receive all of their property being transported upon paying the amount of the ***non-binding*** estimate plus 10%. This rule only applies when the controlling estimate for services is ***non-binding.*** The rule does not apply for ***binding*** cubic feet or other volume-based estimates.

Consumer Protection tip. Always make certain to receive all estimates in writing and make sure all terms are clearly spelled out; never accept verbal promises or guarantees. Estimates must be completed, approved by the customer, and signed BEFORE the moving company begins any work to pack or load the shipment.

Post contract services exception.

The original intent of the 110% Rule was to protect consumer shippers from charges well in excess of the estimate. However, in August 2005 the 110% Rule was amended to include an exception for "post contract services." Consequently, this amendment diminished the power of the 110% Rule, thereby weakening the strength of this very important consumer protection law. As such, the need for moving companies to provide honest and accurate estimates to consumer shippers is more important than ever.

The 110% Rule does not apply to post contract services not listed on the estimate. Those extra or "post contract services" must be ordered separately and paid in advance of the property being unloaded. (49 USC Section 13707(b)(3)(C)) states in pertinent part:

> "Post-contract services. - [The 110% rule] does not apply to additional services requested by a shipper after the contract of service is executed that were not included in the estimate."

It is standard practice for a moving company to offer extra services at an additional charge. An example of extra services not included in the weight or "line-haul" charges are for the use of expedited guaranteed delivery service, stairs, shuttle, long carry, elevator, packing and labor, storage, appliance services, etc. A consumer should have a clear understanding of what services are included in the estimate and what services will be charged at an additional rate. (see chapter 11 for more information)

Samples of Post Contract Services may include:	
Long carry	Shuttle charge
Stairs and/or elevator	Appliance servicing/install
Rigging, hoisting, and lowering	Wooden crating
Storage service	Unpacking/disposal
Re-delivery service	Third party servicing

Consumer alert: Consider the following situation as an example of a worst case scenario where the consumer shipper is required to legally pay almost three times the original estimate. A consumer shipper should be aware and avoid such a scenario; a moving company should take steps to avoid placing a consumer shipper in this situation.

A consumer shipper obtains a non-binding estimate from a moving company based on moving 200 items at an estimated weight of 3,000 lbs. at a cost of $1,500 for a move from Austin, Texas, to Las Vegas, Nevada.

On the scheduled date of pickup the mover arrives and observes that the consumer shipper has increased the number of items to be moved to 400 and not 200 as originally estimated and orders additional services. The moving company, prior to any work beginning, cancels the original estimate and the consumer shipper signs a new "revised non-binding estimate" based on 400 items at an estimated weight of 6,000 lbs. at a cost of $3,000. This new estimate becomes the current estimate from which the 110% Rule would be calculated.

Sometime later, upon arrival at the delivery location the moving company discovers that $1,000 of extra services would be required to complete the move (e.g. $500 shuttle, $200 stairs, and $300 long carry = $1,000 total extra charges). Since these charges were not listed on the estimate they would be classified as "post contract services" and the consumer would be required to pay for those services in advance without the protection of the 110% Rule.

If the weight certificates determined that the actual weight of the property was 7,500 lbs. (7,500 lbs. at $0.50 per lb. = $3,750), then the consumer shipper would legally be required to pay $4,300 to receive their property. The balance due of $450 must be billed after 30 days per the 110% Rule. See the following table of charges:

Original estimate:
3,000 lbs. at $0.50 per lb. = $1,500.00

Revised estimate signed on date of pickup:
6,000 lbs. at $0.50 per lb. = $3,000.00

A revised estimate is issued if the consumer is moving more property than originally estimated. The revised estimate cancels the original estimate. Revised estimates must be approved and signed by the customer before services begin.

Actual weight charges after weighing:
7,500 lbs. at $0.50 per lb. = $3,750.00

Additional post contract charges:
$500 shuttle, $200 stairs, $300 long carry

Post contract charges are additional fees charged for services that were not included on the estimate. These charges must be paid in addition to the moving charges. If the consumer does not pay the additional fees, the company is not required to perform the service.

Total actual charges for all services:	
Actual weight charges: 7,500 lbs.	$ 3,750.00
Shuttle (post contract)	$ 500.00
Stairs (post contract)	$ 200.00
Long carry (post contract)	$ 300.00
Total actual charges: grand total	**$ 4,750.00**

Payment due at delivery before unloading based upon 110% Rule: Revised estimate ($3,000) + 10% ($300) + post contract fees ($1,000) = $4,300	
Total due before unloading:	**$ 4,300.00**
Balance invoiced after 30 days: [3]	**$ 450.00**

[3] Total charges are based upon actual services. Customer must only be required to pay the amount of the last non-binding estimate plus 10% (110% Rule) and any post contract service charges to receive their property. Any remaining balance must be billed 30 days after delivery. See example above ($4,750 - $4,300 = $450 to be billed).

	How a moving company can protect consumers by preventing unexpected increases in charges for services.
☐	Provide consumer shippers with honest and accurate estimates based on a detailed and an accurate item list and services to be performed.
☐	Prior to the moving day provide consumer shipper with a complete explanation and list of all possible accessorial charges.
☐	Prior to the moving day make certain the consumer shipper understands that the price is not guaranteed if additional items are moved or additional services ordered.
☐	Verify the accuracy of the original estimate by contacting the consumer shipper several days prior to the move to confirm the services ordered and find out if any changes have been made to the number of items to be moved or services requested and inform the consumer of any changes to the price.
☐	Regularly monitor the percentage of total moves where the original estimate increased on the day of the move. If original estimates are honest and accurate then the percentage of estimate increases on the day of the move should be relatively low.
☐	Establish a company-wide policy that prevents interline agent carriers to issue a revised written estimate without prior company authorization. By requiring company authorization, management can confirm with the customer that the need for a revised written estimate is legitimate, in compliance with the governing regulations, and that it was approved it in good faith prior to servicing beginning.
☐	If there is a legitimate reason to revise an estimate, make certain to use a revised written estimate form that contains a warning to the consumer shipper not to sign blank documents.

Weight Based Charges

CHAPTER 8

Do moving companies need to determine the weight of a shipment?

Generally, yes. When the moving company transports a non-binding estimate to be charged by weight they must determine the weight of each shipment before they can start charging the consumer shipper. The moving company must provide a written explanation of volume to weight conversions if applicable. (49 CFR section 375.507).

EXCEPTION: When an estimate is provided to the consumer shipper as a "binding cubic feet" estimate and the charges are to be calculated based upon cubic feet, then the law does not require the moving company to obtain weight certificates.

How must moving companies determine the weight of a shipment?

The moving company must use a certified scale. The moving company can choose from the following two methods of weighing.
(49 CFR section 375.509(a)).

Origin Weigh:
The difference between the tare weight of the vehicle before loading at the origin of the shipment and the gross weight of the vehicle after loading the shipment.

Back Weigh:
The difference between the gross weight of the vehicle with the shipment loaded and the tare weight of the vehicle after the moving company unloads the shipment.

What must be done before weighing?

Three conditions must exist for both tare and gross weighings. (49 CFR section 375.509(b)).
1. The vehicle must have installed all equipment required in the transportation of shipment (i.e., ramps, dollies, pads);
2. The driver must be off the vehicle during weighing; and
3. The fuel tanks must be full at the time of weighing. Unless origin weigh is used, in which case the driver must refrain from adding fuel between the two weighings.

May individual consumer shippers observe the weighing?

Generally, yes. The moving company must give the individual shipper the right to observe all weighings of the shipment. They must inform the individual shipper of when the weighing will occur and give them a reasonable opportunity to be present. (49 CFR section 375.513).

Do moving companies need weight tickets?

Generally, yes. For all shipments where charges are determined by the weight (in pounds) of the property, the moving company must obtain a certified weight certificate of the shipment. If a weight certificate is not legal a court may hold it to be invalid and/or the DOT/FMCSA may impose a fine upon the moving company for each invalid weight certificate. For a weight certificate to be legal and valid it must be obtained in compliance with the governing federal regulations. (See 49 CFR §§ 375.501 - 521).

Legal requirements for weight certificates.

Consumer shippers must be advised that they are entitled to observe the weighing. Moving companies must provide the shipper with the location and time of the weighing and a reasonable opportunity for them to be present. (49 CFR § 375.513).

If a consumer shipper disputes the weight of the shipment they have a right to demand a re-weighing of the property at no charge. The actual charges, notwithstanding the 110% rule, must be based on the weight from the re-weighing, regardless if it is higher or lower than the original weight. (49 CFR § 375.517)

A legal weight certificate must contain the following elements:
1. The complete name and location of the scale.
2. The date of each weighing.
3. Identification of the weight as being the tare, gross, or net.
4. The company/carrier vehicle identification number.
5. The name of the shipper as it appears on the bill of lading.
6. The job or order number for the individual shipment.
7. The signature of the weigh master.

A true copy of the weight certificate must be provided to the shipper along with the bill of lading and other shipping documents. The carrier must also retain a copy of the weight certificate in each shipper's file. (49 CFR § 375.519)

Consumer tip. If a consumer shipper disputes the weight of the property they are entitled to observe a free re-weighing of the goods at a certified scale. All parties will be bound by the re-weigh scale results.

Cubic Feet vs. Weight Charges

CHAPTER 9

Charges for moving services may be based on any form of calculation identified in the moving company's published tariff. Generally, charges for interstate shipments of household goods are charged based upon weight or cubic feet or distance or by the hour. There are advantages and disadvantages to each method of charging. A moving company may only calculate charges based on the method(s) identified in its published tariff.

Is charging by cubic feet legal?

Yes, charging a consumer shipper for an interstate move based on cubic feet is legal if the moving company has a provision for cubic feet charges in its tariff and follows the general provisions of the law. Charges based on cubic feet, or other volume-based charges, are allowed if the written estimate is BINDING. Additionally, a moving company may also offer options to a consumer shipper to charge based on weight or cubic feet if the moving company has a published tariff that allows for both options.

Requirements for a moving company to charge by cubic feet.

Federal law under 49 USC Section 14104(b)(1)(C) requires that "non-binding" estimates must be based on weight only. This section does not prohibit charges based on cubic feet; however it limits cubic feet charges to BINDING estimates. Moreover, a moving company must generally follow certain requirements to legally charge a consumer shipper based on cubic feet. The following are requirements for correctly/legally charging a customer based on cubic feet:

1. Estimates based on cubic feet must be BINDING.
2. Estimate must indicate that charges are based on cubic feet.
3. Moving company must have a TARIFF permitting cubic feet.
4. The cubic feet charges must be based on accurate measurements.
5. Moving company may charge a fee for providing a written BINDING estimate.

Collection of Charges

CHAPTER 10

A moving company must issue an honest, truthful freight or expense bill of all rates and charges for the transportation and related services. The charges must be in accordance with the moving company's appropriately published tariff provisions in effect, including the method of payment. (See 49 CFR section 375.215).

A moving company must specify in writing the acceptable forms of payment and other payment terms before services begin.

A moving company must specify the form of payment and when payment is to be tendered. For example, a moving company may wish to require that a $100 non-refundable deposit be paid upon booking; 50% payment upon pickup; and the balance due by credit card on the date of delivery prior to unloading.

To specify the form and time of payment, the moving company must ensure the following:

1. Their tariff specifies the form and time of payment; and
2. The estimate, bill of lading, and order for service all specify the form and manner of payment in writing.

Note: the above rules for collecting payment are subject to the 110% Rule as discussed in chapter 7 of this book.

> **Consumer tip.** Consumer shippers must be informed in writing of the forms of payment acceptable. Consumer shippers must be given written notice that COD shipments must be paid in full prior to unloading. (Subject to the 110% Rule for non-binding estimates). A moving company which stands behind the quality of their services will accept multiple forms of payment at delivery – such as check, credit card, and cash. Be wary of any company that only accepts cash at delivery.

Accessorial Services

CHAPTER 11

Charges for accessorial and third party services.

In addition to providing basic moving services, most moving companies perform a variety of accessorial services. In many cases, accessorial services are not automatically included in the base moving estimate and will only be performed at an additional charge. Each individual moving company will create its own list of accessorial services and determines if the service in offered as an extra charged item or if it is included in the base estimate for service. It should never be assumed that all services are automatically included in the base estimated charges. It is advised that consumers carefully review their estimate to make certain that all required services are included. Moving companies must describe each accessorial service and the charges for such in their interstate tariff.

If the accessorial service is not included in the estimate and the consumer shipper does not pay the extra charge; the moving company is not required to perform the service. Take for example the "long carry" service. Long carry is an accessorial service that some moving companies will only provide at an additional charge. For example, if the delivery truck must park more than 50 to 75 feet away from the front of the residence the moving company will charge a long carry fee to have the crew carry the property from the truck into the home. As such, in this example the moving company would not be required to move the property into the home unless the consumer shipper paid the extra fee. If the consumer shipper does not pay the extra fee, the property will only be offloaded out of the end of the truck, and the consumer shipper would have to move the property into the residence themselves.

The following list contains examples of possible accessorial services that may be charged in addition to the base estimate. Charges for accessorial services vary from company to company. A complete list of services and charges should be provided to the consumer shipper upon request. Consumer shippers should obtain and examine a complete listing of accessorial services and charges before hiring a moving company.

Exclusive use of the vehicle. Oftentimes, a consumer shipper's property will be consolidated with other shipments on the same moving truck. It is not uncommon for two or three different loads of consumers' property to be loaded onto a single moving truck for transport. Consolidating shipments is a common practice to help moving companies maintain efficiency and as a way to keep costs down. If an individual consumer shipper wishes to have their property exclusively occupy the transport vehicle they can request and pay for an "exclusive use of the vehicle" service.

Stairs. Many moving companies will charge a stairs fee for walking the property up a flight of stairs. If a moving company charges for stairs, then the cost will be calculated per step or per flight of stairs. The more steps needed to walk up to your new residence, the higher the charge for stairs will be.

Long carry. If the delivery truck cannot park directly in front of the residence and the crew of movers must carry the property a distance of more than 50 to 75 feet from the truck, then a long carry fee will be assessed to the consumer shipper. Long carry fees are charged based upon the distance from the back of the truck to the residence. The longer the movers need to walk from the truck to the residence the greater the long carry charge will be.

Appliance servicing. Moving companies will offload appliances into the residence but generally will not set up or hook up appliances. If a consumer shipper wishes to have the movers set up a washer, dryer, or other appliance, then an extra appliance servicing fee will be assessed.

Elevator. Similar to the stairs charge, some moving companies may charge an extra fee if they need to load the goods into an elevator to move them to the floor where the residence is located. Moving companies who charge an elevator service fee do so because they claim moving the goods in an elevator delays the entire delivery process.

Storage. Storage of property is not automatically included with moving services unless ordered prior to pickup. Where storage was not anticipated but required by the consumer shipper before the scheduled delivery, an extra fee will be assessed by the moving company. Unanticipated storage charges arise for many different reasons. Most commonly, unanticipated storage is required when the consumer shipper's new home is not ready. Also, unanticipated storage would be necessary if the consumer shipper does not have the funds to pay for the total moving services. If payment for the legitimate moving services is not made, then the moving company can refuse to delivery and place the property into storage at the consumer shipper's expense. Storage fees increase the longer the property is in storage.

Re-delivery. A moving company may charge a re-delivery fee if the consumer shipper is unavailable to receive the property during the first delivery attempt. In such a case, the moving company would have had to place the goods into storage and then made a second or "re-delivery" attempt to make delivery.

Waiting time. If the consumer shipper is not available to meet the delivery truck at the residence on the day of delivery, the moving company may charge a fee for waiting. Fees for waiting may be charged on an hourly or daily basis. The moving company is not required to wait and may choose instead to place the property in storage (at the consumer shipper's expense) and drive on to their next delivery.

Crating. Certain items of property can be better packed and protected in transport by crating the item. Crating is a custom packing service where the item is packed in a form-fitted crate for protection. Generally, crating refers to an item that can be contained in a custom built wooden crate or in cardboard boxes cut apart and form-fitted around the item. The term crating has been used to describe both services.

Third party servicing. Many specialty items require a third party service company to breakdown, pack, and install for maximum protection. Third party companies may be hired at the expense of the consumer shipper to break down, pack, or install such items. Items which may require third party servicing could include: grandfather clocks, large safes, pool tables, hot tubs, workout equipment, etc.

Bulky items. Unusually large and bulky items may require special packing and handling charges. Items such as: canoes, kayaks, hot tubs, pool tables, etc.

Unpacking/disposal. Typically, unpacking of property is not included in moving services. Unpacking services may be available at a fixed fee or on an hourly basis. Additionally, when packing materials such as boxes, bubble wrap, and packing paper are used in the packing of property, those items are the property of the consumer shipper and will not be collected and disposed of by the moving company unless a disposal fee is charged.

Split pickup or delivery. It is not unusual for a consumer shipper to have items picked up or delivered to more than one location. For example, a consumer shipper may wish to have some of their items delivered to their new residence and some of their items moved into a storage unit at a different location. When split pickup or delivery is required, the service will be performed at an additional fee.

Rigging/Hoisting/Lowering. These services are usually accessed when a consumer shipper is moving into an upper level unit of an older building and certain items being moved cannot fit up the staircase into the unit. In such cases a moving company might have to set up a rope and pulley rigging system to raise the item up and into the unit through a window. A moving company is not required to offer this service and will only do so when they have the equipment and expertise to safely perform the service.

Consumer protection tip. An individual moving company may offer any accessorial services they wish at any price they set in their tariff. Accessorial services may vary from company to company. It is advised that when considering the selection of a moving company that the consumer shipper review the list of accessorial services and the charges for each.

Limitation of Liability

CHAPTER 12

Moving companies may legally limit their liability for loss or damages while offering shippers full value protection insurance.

Damaged or lost property is an unfortunate reality when undertaking the complex task of transporting household goods across great distances. Many consumer shippers may expect and accept a reasonable degree of damage. Moving companies also understand that, despite their best efforts in packing and securing property, damage and loss occurs. Damage and loss can be mitigated by the use of proper packing methods and through comprehensive valuation and/or insurance coverage.

An inherent conflict seems to exist between moving companies who wish to substantially limit their liability and shippers who wish to have their property transported with the highest levels of coverage. The competing interests of moving companies and shippers can be overcome by combining both insurance and valuation as a means of providing coverage for damage or loss to property.

Insurance vs. Valuation

To accomplish the win-win situation of limiting the moving company's liability while providing the shipper with full value coverage, it is important to understand the legal distinction between valuation and insurance in the context of interstate transportation of household goods.

Generally, insurance is an agreement where one party assumes a risk faced by another party in return for a premium payment. In most states insurance is regulated and may only be sold by state licensed insurance agents. To legally sell insurance a moving company must issue an actual insurance policy to the shipper identifying the level of coverage and exceptions; have in place a legally published tariff providing for liability insurance coverage; and have the appropriate state license to sell insurance. (49 CFR section 375.303(c)).

Alternatively, when a shipper requests insurance coverage a moving company should refer the shipper to a third-party insurance provider such as Baker Moving Insurance, MovingInsurance.com, or Unirisc, Inc. These entities can help provide the shipper with actual insurance coverage protecting their property from loss or damage. Generally, these entities can provide professional claims representatives and high quality customer service to process the consumer shipper's claims in a more efficient manner.

In comparing valuation to insurance, the primary point to understand is that valuation is not insurance. Valuation is "the degree of worth of the shipment." The valuation charge compensates the moving company for assuming a greater degree of liability than is provided for in its base transportation charges. (49 CFR section 375 appendix A). In practical application, valuation is the memorialization of the agreement between the parties as to the moving company's limitation of liability in the event of any loss or damage. The most common level of valuation coverage is the standard basic liability option of $0.60 per pound per article.

The confusion between insurance and valuation is compounded when moving companies tell shippers that they provide "basic insurance" when in fact they are only providing "basic valuation" of $0.60 per pound per article. Moving companies should be aware that this practice may be classified as statutory insurance fraud and could subject the moving company and the moving company's sales agent to civil and criminal penalties.

In short, it is advised that moving companies not use the word "insurance" when, in fact, they mean to say "valuation."

Generally, moving companies may not release themselves from total liability.

Federal law governing the interstate transportation of household goods generally prohibits a moving company from contracting with the shipper to release itself from all liability. (49 CFR section 375.701(a)). At a minimum the moving company will always be liable for the basic valuation of $0.60 per pound per article for any loss or damaged goods.

This prohibition against global releases of liability presents real-world problems in situations where shippers refuse to have articles wrapped in protective blankets or to purchase professional packing services. Since the law generally makes limited exceptions, the moving company must either undertake the risk of transporting unprotected goods or pack the item despite the shipper's refusal to pay additional packing charges.

Although the above cited federal law prohibits the use of global releases of liability in regard to damaged goods, the use of a release of liability in regard to the damaged *real property* such as floors, walls, ceilings, landscaping, driveways, walkways, etc., may be outside the scope of the federal law restricting the use of liability releases. As such, a moving company could include as a term in the bill of lading a release of liability for damage to such real property.

Other exceptions to the prohibition against releasing a moving company's liability include limiting liability where a shipper packs perishable, dangerous, or hazardous materials without the moving company's knowledge. A shipper who packs such items without the moving company's knowledge may be subject to civil and criminal penalties, including imprisonment for up to five years. (49 USC section 5124).

A moving company will also be released from liability where a shipper fails to notify the moving company by way of written declaration of the items of extraordinary value to be transported. Items of extraordinary value are generally classified as items valued at more than $100 per pound such as jewelry, laptop computers, and other such valuables. Where a shipper fails to declare items of extraordinary value a moving company's liability may be limited to the released value valuation of $0.60 per pound per article. (49 CFR section 375.203(b)).

Full replacement valuation default.

Many moving companies are under the misguided belief that the basic limited liability level of property damage coverage of $0.60 per pound per article is the industry standard default level of protection afforded to shippers. This is not the case. The default level of coverage is not $0.60 per pound per article, but in fact, full replacement value. The default level of valuation becomes effective where moving companies do not take the appropriate legal steps to limit their liability. (49 USC 14706(f)).

Federal law requires that moving companies provide a customer with at least two valuation levels. (49 CFR section 375.203). Generally, the two options are (1) 60 cents per pound per article; and (2) full replacement value. A shipper must be provided with a reasonable opportunity to select between the two choices. If the customer selects "60 cents per pound per article" then certain steps must be taken to make it a legal choice. Failure to correctly follow the requirements will automatically change the selection to full replacement value even if the shipper did not pay additional money for the higher valuation level.

How to legally limit liability to $0.60 per pound per article.

Moving companies may limit their liability, with agreement of the shipper, to the minimum valuation of $0.60 per pound per article. Under this valuation option the moving company assumes liability of no more than $0.60 per pound per article. For example, if a 50 pound plasma TV, valued at $3,000, was lost or destroyed the moving company would be liable for no more than $30. To legally limit its liability to this basic valuation level the moving company must take necessary and specific steps such as:

A. Offer at least two *valuation* options to the shipper. The surface transportation board through its Released Rates of Motor Carrier Shipments of Household Goods has established two different valuation options: (1) Full Value Protection Valuations and (2) Released Value Valuations of $0.60 per pound per article. Both options must be offered to the shipper.

B. Provide the shipper with a reasonable opportunity to select between the options. It is important that shippers be provided a clear choice between the two levels of valuation protections. Generally, a shipper must be provided a copy of the booklet entitled, "Your Rights and Responsibilities When You Move" prior to the signing of an order for service. (49 CFR section 375.213(a)(1)). Additionally, the bill of lading and/or order for service should include a written explanation of the valuation choices as provided by the Surface Transportation Board. (49 CFR sections 375.501(a)(10) and 375.501(a)(12)).

C. The shipper must write in their own handwriting their statement declaring the value of the shipment. To release the shipment to the basic valuation level the shipper must write the words ***"60 cents per pound per article."*** Moving companies should be advised that abbreviations such as "60 ¢ p.p.p.a" or ".60/lbs." do not hold the same force and effect as the writing of the complete phrase: ***"60 cents per pound per article"*** and may not be enforceable in a court of law.

D. Maintain a properly published and up-to-date interstate tariff. (49 USC section 13702(c)(1)). A tariff is a legal document, unique to each moving company, issued in whole or in part which contains the rates, rules, regulations, classifications, terms and conditions by which the interstate transportation of goods is governed. The tariff must be published, maintained, and made available to shippers and representatives of the US DOT/FMCSA upon reasonable request.

E. Issue a proper interstate bill of lading. The bill of lading is the contract of carriage between the moving company and the shipper. Each interstate shipment must be accompanied by a properly formatted bill of lading listing rates and charges corresponding to the applicable tariff provisions. (49 CFR section 375.505).

(See generally: *Allison-Erwin Co. v. Saturn Freight Sys.* 106 F. supp. 2d 1328, 1330 (N.D. Ga. 2000) (quoting *Bio-Lab, Inc. v. Pony Express Courier Corp.*, 911 F.2d 1580, 1582 (11th Cir. 1990)).

Combing valuation and insurance to create a win-win scenario.

As described above, an inherent conflict appears to exist between moving companies that wish to substantially limit their liability and shippers who wish to have their property transported with the highest levels of coverage. The competing interests of moving companies and shippers can be overcome by combining both insurance and valuation as a means of providing coverage for damage or loss to property.

When a shipper purchases full coverage insurance from a third-party insurance agent; the shipper is still required to declare their valuation level to the moving company. The win-win scenario is created when the shipper purchases full coverage insurance and they release the moving company's liability to the limited liability valuation level of $0.60 per pound per article.

Under this scenario should the property be damaged, the shipper will have full replacement coverage insurance, less any deductible, which they purchased from a third-party insurer. The insurer will then exercise its right to subrogation and seek reimbursement from the moving company. The benefit to the moving company is that the third-party insurer exercising its right to subrogation is bound by the valuation selection made by the shipper.

When all the steps are followed a scenario can be created whereby the shipper is fully covered for their lost or damaged goods and the moving company is protected by the $0.60 per pound per article limitation of liability; it's a win-win situation for the shipper and moving company.

Valuation Options

CHAPTER 13

Interstate moving companies are generally liable for damaged or loss of the property being transported. There are two different levels of liability available for consumer shippers to select.

There are generally two different levels of liability moving companies are required to provide to consumer shippers. Under federal law, interstate moving companies must offer two different liability options referred to as valuation coverage: (1) Full Value Protection and (2) Released Value (limited liability).

Full Value Protection and Released Value are not insurance policies governed by state insurance laws; instead, they are federal contractual tariff levels of liability authorized under Released Rates Orders of the Surface Transportation Board of the U.S. Department of Transportation.

(1) Full Replacement Value Protection.

Under Full Replacement Value Protection, an interstate moving company is liable for the replacement value of lost or damaged goods in the entire shipment. This is the most comprehensive valuation option available for the protection of a consumer shipper's property. Under federal law, Full Replacement Value Protection is the default level of valuation coverage.

Unless the consumer shipper waives in writing the Full Replacement Value Protection option and selects an alternative valuation option, a moving company must replace or fully reimburse the consumer shipper for any damage or loss. Under the Full Replacement Value protection option, if any article is lost, destroyed or damaged while in the moving company's custody the company must offer to either (1) repair the item, (2) replace the item with a similar item, or (3) make a cash settlement for the cost of the repair or the current market replacement value.

Under this option, moving companies are permitted to limit their liability for loss or damage to articles of extraordinary value. Consumer shippers must specifically list these articles on the shipping documents to have them covered. An article of extraordinary value is any item with a value that exceeds $100 per pound (i.e., jewelry, rare coins, silverware, china, furs, etc.).

(2) Limited Liability Valuation option of $0.60 per pound per article.

Under the Limited Liability Valuation option, a moving company will only be liable for up to $0.60 per pound per article for any items damaged or lost during an interstate move. For example, if a 10 pound laptop computer valued at $2,000 is lost or destroyed the consumer shipper would only receive $6.00 in compensation ($0.60 x 10 pounds = $6.00). This option is provided free of cost to consumer shippers.

A consumer shipper must be provided with a reasonable opportunity to select between the two choices. If the consumer shipper selects "60 cents per pound per article" then certain steps must be taken to make it a legal choice. Failure to correctly follow the requirements will automatically change the selection to "Full Replacement Value Protection" even if the consumer shipper did not pay additional money for the higher valuation level.

The following are requirements for correctly selecting "$0.60 per pound per article":
1. At least two options must be made available for the consumer shipper. DO NOT cross out the replacement option on the bill of lading.
2. The consumer shipper must write in their own handwriting, the words: ***"60 cents per pound per article."***
3. Abbreviations may not be legal. For example "60 ¢ p.p.p.a"
4. If no selection is made or the full sentence is not correctly written, then Full Replacement Value Protection automatically becomes the selection.

Filing of Claims

CHAPTER 14

Filing of claims.

Consumer shippers are entitled to file claims for loss or damage to property with the moving company issuing the bill of lading. All claims must be filed in accordance with federal law, 49 CFR section 370.3, and must be submitted within the timetable as described on the applicable bill of lading. Claims must be processed in accordance with the valuation option selected by the consumer shipper.

A properly submitted claim must contain the following information:
1. All claims must be submitted to the moving company in written form. Electronic communications are acceptable when agreed to in advance by the shipper and moving company.
2. All claims must be filed within 9 months of delivery of the property.
3. Written claims must contain sufficient facts to identify the specific shipment and items of property.
4. Written claims must assert liability for the alleged loss, damage, injury, or delay.
5. Written claims must include a demand for payment of a specified or determinable amount of compensation.

A moving company may not voluntarily pay a claim unless and until a formal claim in writing for a specified or determinable amount of money has been filed in accordance with the federal requirements. If the claim cannot be processed and disposed of within 120 days after the receipt thereof, the moving company shall at that time, and at the expiration of each succeeding 60 day period while the claim remains pending, advise the claimant in writing of the status of the claim and the reason for the delay.

Processing of claims.

Claims must be acknowledged within 30 days. A moving company must, upon receipt in writing or by electronic transmission of a proper claim, acknowledge the receipt of such claim in writing to the claimant within 30 days after the date of its receipt. The moving company shall indicate in its written acknowledgment to the claimant what, if any, additional documentary evidence or other pertinent information may be required to further process the claim.

Each claim must be assigned a successive claim file number. A moving company must, at the time each claim is received, create a separate file and assign thereto a successive claim file number and note that number on all documents filed in support of the claim and all records and correspondence with respect to the claim, including the acknowledgment of receipt.

Each claim must be date stamped on the date received. On the date each claim is received, the moving company shall stamp the date of receipt on the face of the claim document. The date stamp and successive file number must also be placed and noted on the order for service, bill of lading, the delivery receipt, and any other claim documents.

Investigation of claims.

Each claim received by a moving company must be promptly reviewed and investigated. Investigations shall include reviewing the consumer shipper's claim document and other such supporting material submitted with the claim. When necessary, a claim investigation shall include the review of the bill of lading, order for service, inventory logs, photographs, and other supporting documentation.

Offers of settlement or denial of claims issued within 120 days.

A moving company that receives a properly submitted claim from a consumer shipper must review and investigate the claim and issue a written notice to either pay, decline, or make a firm settlement offer within 120 days after receipt of the claim.

Neutral Arbitration

CHAPTER 15

As with any industry, disputes can arise between a customer and a company. The moving industry is no different. Disputes between a moving company and a consumer shipper can arise for many reasons. The most common disputes a consumer shipper can have with a moving company will involve issues of overcharges for services, failure to deliver on time, or damages and missing items.

Consumer shippers have several options in trying to resolve the disputes with a moving company. The best method for resolving the dispute is direct discussion with moving company customer service department. A legitimate moving company will have a customer service department which can address and help resolve disputes. In most cases, any issues or disputes can be resolved as a matter of customer service. However, when an issue cannot be resolved through the normal customer service methods, a consumer may wish to look to other means to address the issues.

When considering alternative approaches to address and resolve a dispute, a consumer shipper may consider filing a lawsuit, complaining to a consumer watch organization or to a government regulatory agency. Although potentially effective in the long run, those methods may take a great deal of time and could potentially be expensive.

In the interstate moving industry, the FMCSA requires that each moving company have in place a neutral arbitration program to help resolve disputes. Neutral arbitration can serve as a cost effective and quick alternative to traditional litigation. Additionally, neutral arbitration is more informal than court litigation and a consumer shipper may be able to navigate the arbitration process without hiring an attorney.

What is arbitration?

Interstate moving companies must have in place a neutral arbitration program, administered through an independent arbitration service provider. The program must be designed to give neither the moving company nor the consumer shipper any special advantage. Arbitration may provide a faster and more cost-effective method of obtaining a final and binding resolution of a dispute that cannot be resolved through direct or assisted negotiations.

Is arbitration mandatory?

Federal law governing interstate shipments of household goods under 49 CFR § 375.211 provides that an interstate moving company must have a program in place to provide shippers with an arbitration alternative to litigation. Arbitration is optional and not required under federal law. A moving company cannot require that a consumer shipper proceed through arbitration prior to litigation. Arbitration is available for all claims involving property loss, property damage, and disputes over charges for services.

Moving companies must provide written notice of arbitration to shippers.

A moving company must provide each potential consumer shipper with a written summary of the arbitration program prior to the order for service being issued. The written summary of the moving company's arbitration program must include (1) a summary of the arbitration process; (2) the associated cost for each party involved in the arbitration; and (3) the legal effects of an arbitration.

The arbitrator selected by the parties must render a decision within 60 days of the receipt of the written notification of the dispute by the parties. In regard to the applicable costs associated with the arbitration, a moving company cannot require that a consumer shipper be responsible for more than 50% of the cost.

If the arbitration alternative is chosen, then any decision made by the arbitrator may be binding if the dispute is for an amount less than $10,000. Additionally, an arbitration decision may not be appealed in a court of law.

How does the arbitration process begin?

To initiate the arbitration process a consumer shipper simply has to inform the moving company of their intent to arbitrate. It is advised that a demand for arbitration be sent via certified mail to the moving company. Once the moving company has received the written demand for arbitration, they are required to send the proper forms and information from the neutral arbitration service they use. If a moving company fails to comply with the demand for arbitration, they can be sanctioned by the FMCSA with civil penalties.

Sample demand for arbitration letter:

May 6, 2015

XYZ Moving Company
1234 Anywhere Street
Any City, USA 55555

Re: Demand for Neutral Arbitration
Job Order No: XXXXXX

Gentlemen,

Please accept this letter in compliance with United States federal law under 49 USC Section 14708 as a demand for neutral arbitration. As a licensed interstate moving company of household goods, you are required to submit to neutral arbitration for any claims up to $10,000.00. Claims may be made to resolve disputes involving overcharges, damage or loss to goods, and/or failure to make delivery.

This letter will serve as formal demand for neutral arbitration. You are required to send to me written documentation regarding your neutral arbitration service provider and a summary of the arbitration process. You must also send me all the forms necessary to initiate the arbitration process as explained in 49 CFR Section 375.211.

Please send the requested documentation to the following address:

Customer name
Mailing address
City/State/Zip

Your failure to comply with this demand may result in a regulatory action against you by the FMCSA which can result in the revocation of your license.

Respectfully,

Mr./Ms. Customer

Interstate Tariffs

CHAPTER 16

What is a tariff and why must a moving company publish one?

A tariff is a legal document that must be published by every interstate moving company. The tariff specifies the exact prices, services, rules, regulations, classifications, policies, and other provisions of the services offered by the moving company. A moving company is bound by the terms of its published tariff; it must only provide the ***exact services and prices*** as listed in the tariff.

How must a moving company use a tariff?

Moving companies must charge customers the ***exact*** rates from the tariff. No services may be offered to a customer which are not provided for in the tariff. A moving company may not charge a customer ***more or less*** than the specific tariff rate. All charges for services provided to a customer must exactly match the rates of the tariff. For example, if the tariff price for 1,400 lbs. for a move from California to Florida is $0.50 per pound then the moving company must charge exactly $0.50; not one cent more nor one cent less. (49 USC section 13702(a)(2)).

Must the tariff be filed with the US DOT?

Federal law does not require that a moving company file or have the tariff approved by the U.S. Department of Transportation (US DOT) if the tariff is limited to services performed in the 48 contiguous states. However, the law does require that the tariff be published and made available to any shipper who makes a reasonable request to view it. Additionally, tariffs must be kept updated and available to any representative of the US DOT who makes a request to view it. Moving companies must provide written notice to customers of the availability of the tariff. (49 CFR section 375.213(a)(3)).

How may a moving company publish a tariff?

Moving companies may write their own tariff, subscribe to a generic tariff service, or have an individual custom made tariff written for them by a legal professional. Any tariff must be written to comply with all applicable federal regulations. Since a moving company must only provide the exact services and prices as listed in the tariff, it is important that the tariff be made to match the services and prices that the moving company is providing or will provide. Be cautious of generic tariffs that may not exactly match the services and rates the moving company is offering.

If a moving company uses a generic tariff which only allows for line haul charges based on weight of the property, then charging based upon cubic feet would be both a civil and criminal violation. Also, if a generic tariff does not contain provisions for charges for stairs, long carry, storage, etc., then the moving company who uses the generic tariff cannot charge the consumer shipper for those services.

A moving company's published Tariff must match the shipping documents: The terms and conditions written in a moving company Tariff must be identical to the terms and conditions written on the shipping documents such as the bill of lading. Therefore, the same company that helps publish the Tariff should also create the matching shipping documents

Must each moving company have an individual tariff?

The Surface Transportation Board has ruled that effective January 1, 2008, interstate moving companies are not immune from collective rate-making (collective tariff-making). The end to this immunity may subject interstate moving companies to anti-trust prosecution for operating collectively with other moving companies using the same tariff. Effectively, to avoid anti-trust prosecution each moving company should have their own tariff published. Each moving company should publish a tariff with their own table of rates, charges, terms, and conditions.

Can tariff prices be discounted?

No. Tariff rates/prices for line haul and accessorial services must **NOT** be randomly or individually discounted. Moving companies may not charge or receive different rates/prices for services other than the rates/prices specified in the tariff. This includes offering a discount or returning part of the rate to a customer. However, amendments or changes to tariff rates/prices, properly documented, may be used to change the rates/prices for services; this is the only form of "*discounting*" that may be permissible. Under this method careful record keeping must be used to follow the law. 49 USC section 13702(a)(2) states in pertinent part:

> The carrier may not charge or receive a different compensation for the transportation or service than the rate specified in the tariff, whether by returning a part of that rate to a person, giving a person a privilege, allowing the use of a facility that affects the value of that transportation or service, or another device.

Can a moving company replace their current tariff for a custom made tariff individually published?

Yes. If a moving company wishes to replace a generic tariff for a custom made individually published tariff it may do so at anytime. Using a custom made individually published tariff allows a moving company to offer the services it wishes at the rates/prices it needs to charge in order to provide better customer service.

What are the civil and criminal penalties for tariff violations?

Penalties for violating tariff provisions by either ***overcharging or undercharging*** are both civil and criminal. Any person who charges rates over or under the tariff rate shall be liable for a civil penalty of up to $100,000.00 for each individual violation. A person who charges a rate/price ***over or under*** the tariff rate/price may be subject to criminal charges and financial fine and/or a sentence to prison for up to 2 years for ***each*** individual violation. 49 USC section 14903 states in pertinent part:

> (a) Civil Penalty for Undercharging and Overcharging. - A person that offers, grants, gives, solicits, accepts, or receives by any means transportation or service provided for property by a carrier … at a rate different than the [tariff] rate in effect … is liable … for a civil penalty of not more than $100,000 for each violation.
>
> (b) General Criminal Penalty. - A carrier providing transportation or service… or an officer, director, receiver, trustee, lessee, agent, or employee of a corporation… that willfully does not observe its tariffs … shall be fined … or imprisoned not more than 2 years, or both.

Is the moving company responsible if an agent violates a tariff provision?

Yes. Moving companies who use agents or subcontractors, such as other carriers, to perform services can be held civilly and criminally liable for the actions of those agents. For example, if an agent or a subcontractor hired by a moving company to perform a pickup or delivery charges for a service at a rate/price different than the rate specified in the principal moving company's tariff, then the moving company can be held responsible for the violation both criminally and civilly. (49 USC section 14903(c)).

Interstate Shipping Documents

CHAPTER 17

All interstate shipping documents must be in compliance with the FMCSA regulations and filled out completely and accurately. As the laws governing the industry are changed or updated by the FMCSA; updated versions of the documents may be necessary. Motor carriers should update their shipping documents as the regulations change. It is advised that before the start of each moving season motor carriers should check if new versions of the documents are available.

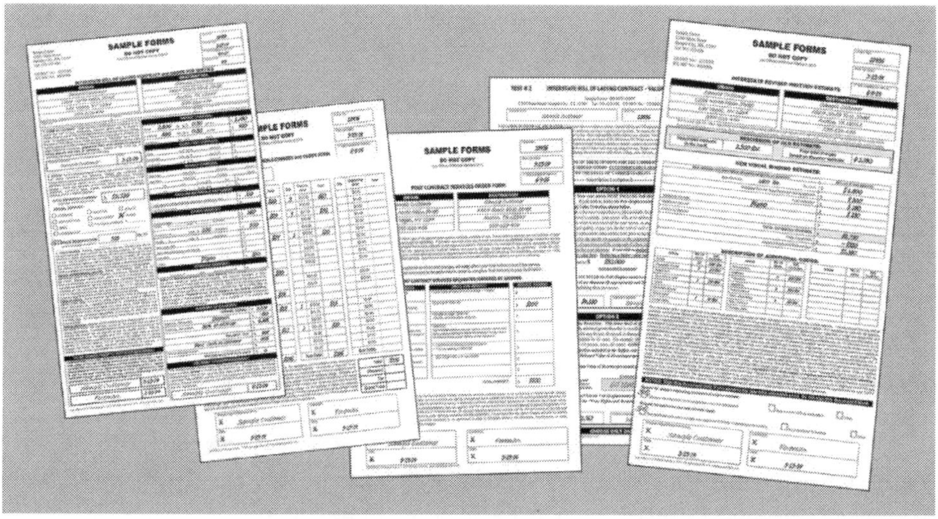

All shipping documents must be filled out completely and correctly. Customers must be provided a complete copy of each document for their records.

Can a consumer shipper be required to sign blank or incomplete documents?

A consumer should ***never*** sign a blank document. In some cases it is ok to sign an incomplete document. An estimate for moving services is not a contract or a guarantee. Since the final charges for the moving services cannot be determined until after the goods have been loaded and weighed (when based upon weight) some of the documents a consumer shipper is required to sign at origin will be incomplete and not contain the final charges. Federal law governing interstate moving specifically states in 49 CFR Section 375.501(d):

> (1) [The motor carrier] may provide the individual shipper with blank or incomplete estimates, orders for service, bills of lading, or any other blank or incomplete documents pertaining to the move.
>
> (2) You may require the individual shipper to sign an incomplete document at origin provided it contains all relevant shipping information except the actual shipment weight and any other information necessary to determine the final charges for all services performed.

It is not unusual for a consumer shipper to be required to sign shipping documents at origin that are incomplete and do not contain the final charges – but do contain all relevant shipping information. However, the estimate or revised written estimate must ***never*** be signed blank or incomplete. The estimate or revised written estimate must contain a detailed itemization of all services and charges and must be approved and signed by the consumer shipper **before services begin.** The estimate or revised written estimate must never be signed blank or incomplete. A consumer shipper should never sign an estimate or revised written estimate that does not list the total estimated charges.

Shipping documents to be provided to consumers include, but are not limited to following:

Written estimate (binding or non-binding): The shipping estimate, under 49 CFR Section 375.401, is a written document itemizing the total estimated charges for the anticipated move.

When an estimate is issued by an interstate broker it is based off of the published tariff of the motor carrier who will perform the transportation service. When an interstate carrier agrees to perform an interstate move based upon the estimate issued by the broker, the carrier agrees to adopt the broker's estimate as their own.

The estimate must be issued as either "binding" or "non-binding" and must specify the form of payment which the company will accept from the customer, must contain all the pertinent pricing and delivery information, and must be signed by both the customer and a representative from the carrier. Estimates must be based upon a visual inspection of the consumer's property unless the consumer's pick up location is more than 50 miles from the carrier's location or if the consumer waives their legal right to a visual inspection of the property in writing.

Estimates must be based upon the terms, conditions, and price formulas from the carrier's published tariff. Estimates should contain unambiguous terms and conditions, and explain to the consumer what is and what is not included in the estimated price. The more accurate information the consumer is provided up front, the less uncertainty will be caused during and after the move. An estimate should also contain a complete menu of all potential accessorial charges that could incur for services ordered by the consumer that were not originally anticipated in the estimate. A consumer should be advised in advance of any and all potential additional service charges.

Rights and Responsibilities when you move booklet and Ready to Move Pamphlet: The FMCSA has published consumer publications helping to explain to consumers the regulations surrounding an interstate move. The Rights and Responsibilities when you move booklet and Ready to Move Pamphlet must be provided to the consumer in advance of issuing an Order for Service. 49 CFR Section 375.213. The Rights and Responsibilities when you move booklet and Ready to Move Pamphlet contain important information that will help inform the consumer of the unique regulations and intricacies involving an interstate move. Carriers should provide the publications in as many days in advance of the move as possible so the customer has time to review the publications thoroughly.

Order for Service: The Order for Service is document which authorizes the carrier to transport the household goods. 49 CFR Section 375.501. "The order for service is not a contract." 49 CFR Section 375 app. A, subpart E. Only the "bill of lading" is a contract for services between the customer and the carrier. The order for service and bill of lading may be combined as one document. 49 CFR Section 375.505(a). Both the customer and the carrier must sign and approve a fully itemized Order for Service in advance of the move beginning.

Bill of lading: The bill of lading is the controlling contract between the shipper and the carrier; it should reflect a complete itemized list of all the actual charges and payments. The bill of lading is the customer's receipt of the transaction and must contain a detailed itemization of the actual charges incurred for the services performed. The order for service and bill of lading may be combined as one document. 49 CFR Section 375.505(a).

Revised Written Estimate: The revised written estimate is an important shipping document that must only be used when the customer changes their order for moving services after the original written estimate has been issued, but before moving services have begun. Changes could include ordering additional services or moving additional items.

A revised written estimate should only be used in circumstances where the customer has made substantial changes to their order for moving services; it should not be used for every move or as part of your regular business model. Most importantly, in the cases where a revised written estimate is necessary, the customer must be given a fully itemized copy of the document listing the new total estimated price and additional services. Moving services may only begin after the customer has reviewed, approved, signed, and given a copy the revised written estimate.

In accordance with 49 CFR § 305.403(a)(6)(ii) and/or 49 CFR § 305.405(b)(7)(ii): If prior to or on the day of the scheduled pick-up the shipper tenders more property or makes a change to the initial order for which they received an estimate; the carrier may either (1) undertake the job with the additional property, in which case the shipper would only be required to pay 10% more than the initial estimate to receive the property on a non-binding estimate or 100% of the binding estimate and the remaining balance will be billed after the 30 day deferment. Or (2) the carrier and shipper may execute a Revised/Rescission document, PRIOR TO LOADING OR OTHERWISE BEGINNING THE JOB, this rescission document and new estimate given prior to loading will serve as the only active estimate for which charges will be calculated.

Inventory logs: Each interstate shipment must include a written itemized inventory log for all goods to be transported by the carrier. The inventory must itemize each box, carton, furniture, or misc. item included in the shipment. 49 CFR Section 375.503. Every item loaded on the vehicle must be assigned an inventory number and its condition at origin documented. Upon delivery, the inventory item numbers are to be used to confirm that each item arrived. The consumer must be given the opportunity to document on the inventory logs the condition of the item as it arrives for delivery. The inventory logs must be signed at origin and again at destination by the consumer and the carrier.

Neutral arbitration disclosure: Interstate moving companies are required to participate in neutral arbitration programs that the consumer may avail themselves of in the event of a conflict involving the final price for services, or damage and/or missing items. A concise easy to read summary of the information concerning the neutral arbitration program must be disclosed to the consumer in writing in accordance with 49 CFR Section 375.211.

Post contract services order form: These optional services are sometimes not included in the estimate and must be ordered by the customer and paid for separately. It is the consumer's option to order any of these services at an additional charge. Under 49 USC 13707(b)(3)(C) a consumer may not be forced to purchase post contract services. For example if long carry is necessary to deliver the property into the home, then this optional service must be ordered and paid in full prior to that service to be performed.

Valuation form: The valuation form as part of the bill of lading contains the valuation information as required by the STB. This important document allows the customer to select between the default full value protection valuation or waive full value and select the limited liability of $0.60 per pound per article.

A moving company's published Tariff must match the shipping documents: The terms and conditions written in a moving company Tariff must be identical to the terms and conditions written on the shipping documents such as the bill of lading. Therefore, the same company that helps publish the Tariff should also create the matching shipping documents

Carrier Operations

CHAPTER 18

May moving companies use subcontracted agents to perform pickup, transportation, storage, or delivery services?

Yes. The primary moving company who booked the job may legally subcontract out the job to another properly licensed moving company to perform part or all of the services. (49 CFR section 375.205).

If the primary moving company wishes to use the services of a subcontracted agent then they must ensure the following:
1. The agent is properly licensed and insured.
2. All contracts with the shipper are written in the name of the primary moving company.
3. An agency agreement exists between the two companies.
4. The agency agreement must be kept on file for at least 24 months.
5. The shipper/customer is informed of the name of the agent, when known.

Information that a moving company must provide to its customers:

Moving companies must provide the following six documents to their consumer shippers before signing an order of service. (49 CFR section 375.213(a)).

Information that a moving company must provide to its customers:
1. The booklet entitled, "Your Rights and Responsibilities When You Move."
2. A concise, easy-to-read, accurate estimate of the moving company's charges.
3. A notice of the availability of the moving company's tariff for the estimate of charges, including an explanation that individual shippers are entitled to copies.
4. A concise, easy-to-read, accurate summary of the moving company's arbitration program.
5. A concise, easy to read, accurate summary of the moving company's customer complaint and inquiry handling procedures, which includes: (i) The moving company's main telephone number that the customer can call; and (ii) A clear and concise statement concerning who must pay for telephone calls; and
6. The pamphlet entitled "Ready to Move." (49 USC 14104(b)(2).

Can someone under 21 years old drive an interstate moving truck?

No. Drivers of interstate moving trucks must be at least 21 years old to drive the vehicle across state lines. This rule applies to any moving truck with a gross vehicle weight (GVW) of over 10,000 pounds.

Note: a driver under 21 years old may be able to operate a moving truck for intrastate (within a single state) moves depending on the individual state laws.

General qualifications for drivers.

A person may not operate a moving truck with a gross vehicle weight (GVW) of over 10,000 pounds across state lines unless they meet the general requirements listed in 49 CFR § 391.11 *et al.*

Requirements for drivers are paraphrased generally as follows:
1. Are at least 21 years old.
2. Can read and speak English.
3. Can safely operate the motor vehicle.
4. Are physically qualified to drive.
5. Have a currently valid driver's license.
6. Have provided a list of violations or certificate (see § 391.27).
7. Are not disqualified to drive (see § 391.15).
8. Have successfully completed a road test (see § 391.31).

Driver's files.

The FMCSA requires that each moving company maintain a driver's qualification file for each driver operating a motor vehicle. A driver's file needs to be kept updated and complete at all times.

A complete driver's qualification file would include the following items:
1. Application for employment (49 CFR section 391.21).
2. Previous employer information request letter (49 CFR section 391.23).
3. DMV record/report (49 CFR section 391.23).
4. Medical exam certificate (medical card) (49 CFR section 391.43(h)).
5. Driver's license copy (49 CFR section 391.33).
6. Annual review of driving record (49 CR section 391.25(c)).
7. List of violations (49 CFR section 391.27).
8. Annual DMV record (49 CFR section 391.25(a)).

Accident registers.

All moving companies are required to maintain a current "accident register" listing all qualifying accidents.

What qualifies as an "accident?"

Not all fender benders qualify as accidents which need to be reported on the "accident register." Only qualifying accidents need to be reported. An accident which qualifies to be reported on the accident register is one that results in. (see 49 CFR section 390.5).

1. A fatality; or
2. Injury to a person requiring medical attention more than mere first aid; or
3. Damage to any vehicle requiring it to be towed from the scene.

Information to be written on an accident register:
1. Date and time of accident.
2. Driver name.
3. Location of accident
4. Number of injuries, if any.
5. Number of fatalities, if any.
6. Whether hazardous materials were involved or were released.

ACCIDENT REGISTER

File	Date and time of Accident	Location of Accident	Vehicle Number	Driver's name	Number of injuries	Number of Fatalities	Police Report No.	Hazardous Materials
1.								
2.								
3.								
4.								
5.								
6.								
7.								
8.								
9.								
10								

Hours of service rules.

Property carrying commercial motor vehicle drivers hours of service regulations
11-Hour Driving Limit: May drive a maximum of 11 hours after 10 consecutive hours off duty.
14-Hour Limit: May not drive beyond the 14th consecutive hour after coming on duty, following 10 consecutive hours off duty. Off-duty time does not extend the 14-hour period.
Rest Breaks: May drive only if 8 hours or less have passed since end of driver's last off-duty or sleeper-berth period of at least 30 minutes. [49 CFR 397.5 mandatory "in attendance" time may be included in break if no other duties performed]
60/70-Hour Limit: May not drive after 60/70 hours on duty in 7/8 consecutive days. A driver may restart a 7/8 consecutive day period after taking 34 or more consecutive hours off duty. Must include two periods from 1 a.m. to 5 a.m. home terminal time, and may only be used once per week, or 168 hours, measured from the beginning of the previous restart.
Sleeper Berth Provision: Drivers using the sleeper berth provision must take at least 8 consecutive hours in the sleeper berth, plus a separate 2 consecutive hours either in the sleeper berth, off duty, or any combination of the two.

FMCSA "Imminent Hazard" Out-of-Service orders

Whenever it is determined that an imminent hazard exists as a result of the transportation by motor vehicle, the FMCSA may order a commercial motor vehicle or employee operating such vehicle out-of-service, or order an employer to cease all or part of the employer's commercial motor vehicle operations. See 49 CFR Section 386.72 *et al.*

"Imminent hazard" means the existence of a condition that presents a substantial likelihood that death, serious illness, severe personal injury, or a substantial endangerment to health, property, or the environment may occur before a notice of investigation proceeding, or other administrative hearing or formal proceeding, to abate the risk of harm can be completed.

Motor Carriers who receive an imminent hazard out-of-service order must cease all interstate transportation services. To successfully reverse an imminent hazard out-of-service order the motor carrier must create a detailed corrective action plan, safety management plan, and file for a formal review of the order.

How long must you keep your records?

The DOT/FMCSA regulations require that a moving company must keep certain records/file in their office for certain periods of time. These files must be made available to representatives of the US DOT/FMCSA upon request. At a minimum a moving company must keep records for the time period specified in the chart on page 107.

An interstate moving company may wish to keep the records/files for a longer period of time for tax purposes or to assist in defending against potential litigation. In many jurisdictions a customer can bring a lawsuit for damages to property up to 2 years from the date of delivery. Consequently, even though the moving company is only required to keep a bill of lading on file for 1 year, it would be necessary to have the bill of lading longer than the 1 year minimum time frame to help defend against a potential lawsuit.

Driver Files/Safety Records:	Retention	Citation
Driver application	During and 3 years after employment	49 CFR § 391.21
DMV record	During and 3 years after employment	49 CFR § 391.23
Road test or DCL	During and 3 years after employment	49 CFR § 391.33
Driver's medical card	During and 3 years after employment	49 CFR § 391.43(h)
Annual review	During and 3 years after employment	49 CFR §§ 391.25; .27
Log books; duty status	6 months after delivery	49 CFR § 395.8(k)
Accident report	3 years	49 CFR § 379.7; Appen. A.

Carrier Files:	Retention	Citation
Agent agreements	2 years after termination of agreement	49 CFR § 375; Appen. A.

Shipper Files:	Retention	Citation
Bills of lading and releases	1 year	49 CFR § 379.7; Appen. A.
Estimate of charges	1 year	49 CFR § 379.7; Appen. A.
Order of service	1 year	49 CFR § 379.7; Appen. A.
Vehicle load manifest	1 year	49 CFR § 379.7; Appen. A.
Descriptive inventory	1 year	49 CFR § 379.7; Appen. A.
*Receipt for R&R Booklet	3 years	49 CFR § 371.111(d)
*Receipt for Ready to Move pamphlet	3 years	49 CFR § 371.111(d)

***Note:** If a consumer consents to receive a copy of the *Rights and Responsibility* booklet and *Ready to Move* pamphlet by electronic delivery the carrier and/or broker must keep a signed receipt indicating the consumer's consent for a period of three years.

Moving Brokers

CHAPTER 19

The information in this chapter focuses on the role, regulations and operations of interstate brokers. Interstate brokers have been described as the middlemen between motor carriers and the consumer shippers and/or the shipping public.[4] Generally, interstate household goods brokers provide estimates for household goods transportation services to potential consumer shippers.

As in many industries there is a spectrum of interstate brokers who provide a variety of service levels at varying quality. At the lower end of the spectrum are the brokers who skirt the law and offer substandard services to consumers. On the high end of the spectrum are top quality professional brokers who operate in full compliance with all regulations, provide consumers with honest and accurate estimates, act as the consumer's advocate during the entire move, and ensures that the moving company acts in honestly, professionally, and honors the terms of the estimate issued to the consumer shipper.

Top quality professional Interstate brokers, when acting in their true capacity as the consumer shipper's agent, can benefit consumer shippers by assuming the role of a consumer advocate, vetting potential motor carriers before the move, acting as the liaison with the motor carrier during the move, and assisting the consumer shipper in resolving claims/complaints with the motor carrier after the move.

Consumer protection Tip. Interstate brokers of household goods must disclose in writing to each consumer shipper that they are acting in the capacity of a broker and are not liable for the acts or omissions of the moving company.

---

[4] See *Reiter v. Cooper*, 507 U.S. 258, 113 Ct. 1213, 122 L. Ed. 2d 604 (1993).

Consumer shippers could benefit from the services of a licensed broker operating in full compliance with the governing regulations in many ways including:

(1) An interstate broker is the consumer shipper's agent and advocate. Interstate brokers can educate and guide consumer shippers through the moving process and ensure that an accurate estimate is issued.

(2) An interstate broker's large client base and volume of business allows individual customers to benefit from competitive pricing.

(3) Interstate brokers acting as the consumer shipper's advocate will research, pre-qualify, and recommend moving companies that are properly licensed and insured.

(4) An interstate broker is the consumer shipper's advocate and can act as the liaison with the moving company on issues of pricing, special services, or claims.

(5) An interstate broker's quality assurance procedures will follow up with customers prior to the scheduled pick up to verify the accuracy of the estimate.

(6) An interstate broker can arrange and recommend third party specialty packing service providers.

Summary Interstate broker regulations

An interstate household goods broker's operations and interactions with consumer shippers and motor carriers are governed by a variety of federal regulations and different federal agencies. The broad scope of regulations, by different federal agencies, creates a challenge in understanding how the different regulations and agencies interact.

The primary licensing entity and regulatory body is the Federal Motor Carrier Safety Administration (FMCSA), which is a subset of the United states Department of Transportation. This agency sets out the licensing requirements, and the majority of regulations governing how the broker conducts business.

In addition to the FMCSA, an interstate broker's operations are also governed by the Surface Transportation Board (STB) and the enforced by the United States Department of Justice. Generally, the STB governs the formation of tariffs, the rates charged, and tariff rate adjustments provided to consumer shippers. Although, an interstate broker does not publish a tariff of its own its operations are dependent upon the terms and conditions and rates of the published tariffs of the motor carriers who will perform the transportation service. Accordingly, an interstate broker must follow the STB regulations in its use of the motor carrier's tariff to quote rates to consumer shippers.

Two milestone changes to the regulations have changed interstate broker's operations and interactions with consumer shippers and motor carriers.

Effective date: January 1, 2008
Agency: Surface Transportation Board

Regulation	Effect on Industry
The Surface Transportation Board in regulating the use of interstate tariffs ended the anti-trust immunity for collective rate-making.[5]	The effect of the decision was that interstate carriers could no longer share tariffs. Each interstate motor carrier was required to publish their own unique tariff of rates and charges without coordination with other competing motor carriers.

Effective date: January 28, 2011
Agency: FMCSA

Regulation	Effect on Industry
The FMCSA updates 49 CFR §371 et seq. governing the operations of interstate household goods brokers and their relationship with potential consumer shippers.	Generally, the regulations govern the overall operations of brokers; disclosures to be made to consumer shippers; and the legal relationships with motor carriers. Perhaps the most important change was that interstate brokers were required to book each move based upon the tariff of the motor carrier who would be performing the service.

[5] Surface Transportation Board Decision, Ex Parte No. 656

Most recently, the regulations governing interstate brokers were also expanded to include an increased surety bond of $75,000.00 and additional registration requirements and penalties for violations.[6]

When acting in compliance with the FMCSA regulations governing their operations; interstate household goods brokers must:

(1) Prominently and unambiguously advertise its services as an interstate household goods broker to potential consumer shippers;[7]

(2) Maintains detailed records of the services, financial transactions, and relationships with the motor carriers within its network;[8]

(3) Works with a network of motor carriers who have been thoroughly vetted, licensed, insured, and disclosed to all potential consumer shippers;[9]

(4) Contracts in writing with each individual motor carrier in its network to offer services and quote rates based upon the published tariff of the individual motor carrier transporting the consumer shipper's property;[10]

(5) Maintains a $75,000.00 surety bond;[11]

(6) Informs and educates consumer shippers of the intricacies of interstate moving and of their legal rights and responsibilities during an interstate move;[12]

---

[6] Moving Ahead for Progress in the 21st Century (MAP-21), Pub. L. No. 112-141 (July 6, 2012).
[7] See 49 CFR § 371.107
[8] See 49 CFR § 371.3
[9] See 49 CFR § 371.105; and § 371.109
[10] See 49 CFR § 371.113(b); and § 375.409
[11] See 49 CFR § 387.307(a)
[12] See 49 CFR § 371.111

(7) Prominently and unambiguously inform potential consumer shippers of the terms and conditions of the contract for services – including deposit, refund, and cancelation policies.[13]

A detailed summary of the January 28, 2011 updates to 49 CFR § 375 *et seq.,* as adopted by the FMCSA, including compliance measures is explained in detail in the following charts.

Summary of Rule	Compliance
49 CFR §371.105: Use of Licensed Motor Carriers: Each motor carrier that works with a broker, via 409 agreement, must have a valid and active FMCSA license to transport household goods.	Broker and carrier must enter into an agreement for services which specifics the terms and conditions of the relationship – in particular that the jobs will be booked from the motor carrier's tariff and that the motor carrier will accept the booked job as if it were their own estimate. Broker should have a current policy in place which screens a motor carrier to verify the active status of the license. Brokers continue to be held liable if a job is sold to a motor carrier who does not have an active license.

Summary of Rule	Compliance
Brokers bond increased to $75,000.	Have a $75,000 surety bond on file with the FMCSA.

Summary of Rule	Compliance
49 CFR § 371.113(b): Estimates must be issued based upon Motor Carrier's Tariff.	Federal law mandates that the broker "must base [the] estimate upon the published tariffs of the authorized motor carrier who will transport the shipper's household goods."

[13] See 49 CFR § 371.117

Summary of Rule	Compliance
49 CFR § 371.107: Advertising Disclosures: In all advertisements, websites, etc. the following information must be ***"prominently"*** displayed: (a) the physical address of where business is conducted. (b) the newly issued DOT ***and*** MC numbers. (c) a statement describing your services as a broker. (d) a statement concerning the use of carrier's tariff. (e) only show logs of carrier's who you have a 409 agreement with.	The FMCSA has purposefully included the term "prominently displayed" in describing how the information on the website must be included. This means that the information may not be in small print or hidden in the terms and conditions. **Statement to be added to all websites:** *"A properly licensed interstate broker is not a motor carrier and will not transport an individual shipper's household goods, but will coordinate and arrange for the transportation of household goods by an FMCSA authorized motor carrier, whose charges will be determined by its published tariff. All estimated charges and final actual charges will be based upon the carrier's tariff which is available for inspection from the carrier upon reasonable request."*

Summary of Rule	Compliance
49 CFR § 371.115: Additional information to be included in 409 agreements.	409 agreements must be kept on file for as long as you are working with the carrier and three years after you stop working with the carrier. 409 agreements are now matters of public record and must be produced for review by any member of the public who wants to see it.

Summary of Rule	Compliance
49 CFR § 371.109: List of Motor Carriers Used: A broker must provide a list of all authorized motor carriers used including their MC and DOT numbers. The list must also include a statement describing that the broker is not an authorized motor carrier.	A complete list of all carrier's must be provided to each potential shipper. The list may be sent to the customer either via: (1) e-mail, or (2) written paper, or (3) listed on the website. **Statement to be included with the list:** *"A properly licensed interstate broker is not a motor carrier and will not transport an individual shipper's household goods, but will coordinate and arrange for the transportation of household goods, and additional services, by an FMCSA authorized motor carrier."*

Summary of Rule	Compliance
Visual in-home Estimate and 50 mile rule Exception: Visual in-home estimates are required if the pick-up location is located within 50 miles of the ***carrier and/or broker's*** headquarters. A written waiver may be placed on the front of the estimate, signed by the customer, waiving their right to receive an in-home estimate. The signed waiver (estimate) must be kept for three years.	If a consumer shipper decided not to have an in-home estimate, then the following waiver must be included on the front of the estimate. **Waiver statement to be placed on estimates:** *"Physical survey waiver agreement: In accordance with 49 CFR §371.113(c)(1), shipper agrees to waive a physical survey of the household goods and alternatively agrees to receive a BINDING estimate based upon the shipper provided item list of property to be transported."* **Note:** Font size of the text on the estimate and terms and conditions must be larger than 7pt. and must be written in the font typeface "Universe."

Summary of Rule	Compliance
Required consumer protection booklets to be given to shippers: Each consumer shipper must be provided a copy of both: (1) the Ready To Move" pamphlet and, (2) the Rights and Responsibilities When you Move" booklet.	The booklets may be provided to the consumer shipper ***either*** by hard copy ***or*** by e-mailing them a link to the FMCSA website PDF file. An actual signature must be kept on file for three (3) years signifying that the customer received the hyperlink to the booklets. You choose to obtain the signature **either** on the estimate itself or on a separate document. If you choose to e-mail the customer a link to the FMCSA website, then the signed estimate must include the following statement: *"I have agreed to receive and subsequently received the FMCSA publications "Ready to Move? – Tips for a Successful Interstate Move" and "Your Rights and Responsibilities When you Move" via e-mail hyperlink and accessed the Federal consumer protection information in the Internet."*

Summary of Rule	Compliance
Disclosure of Refund and Cancellation policy: the company refund cancellation and deposit policy must be written and displayed "prominently" on the website as well as on terms and conditions.	Written request to cancel or have the deposit refunded must be kept for three years.

Broker record keeping requirements

Interstate brokers are required to compile and maintain detailed records in the form of a "master list" delineating all transactions with consumers, the associated motor carrier, the charges for the services, and compensation to the broker.[14] The "master list" must be kept current and produced upon request by any representative of the U.S. DOT – including but not limited to the FMCSA or STB[15]. Federal law under 49 CFR Section 371.3(b) requires that the "master list" be kept for a period of three years and contain the following information:

(1) The name and address of the consignor;

(2) The name, address, and registration number of the originating motor carrier;

(3) The bill of lading or freight bill number;

(4) The amount of compensation received by the broker for the brokerage service performed and the name of the payer;

(5) A description of any non-brokerage service performed in connection with each shipment or other activity, the amount of compensation received for the service, and the name of the payer; and

(6) The amount of any freight charges collected by the broker and the date of payment to the carrier.

---

[14] See 49 CFR § 371.3

[15] Surface Transportation Board

Liability of interstate brokers:

Are interstate brokers liable for the acts or omission of moving companies?

Generally, interstate brokers of household goods are not liable for the acts or omissions of the moving company. A broker provides an estimated cost of services to a potential consumer shipper. A common misconception is that the interstate broker hires or subcontracts the motor carrier on behalf of the consumer shipper. This is not the case.

An interstate broker acts as the agent of the consumer shipper by researching and pre-qualifying a licensed and insured motor carrier who can provide the service the customer is requesting. The interstate broker brings the two parties (consumer shipper and motor carrier) together.

If the consumer shipper hires the motor carrier, then the consumer shipper and the motor carrier enter into a direct contract for moving services. The contract for moving services between the consumer shipper and the motor carrier is called the "bill of lading."[16] The interstate broker is not a party to that contract.

In 1993, the United States Supreme Court described interstate brokers as middlemen between motor carriers [moving companies] and the shipping public. See *Reiter v. Cooper*, 507 U.S. 258, 113 Ct. 1213, 122 L. Ed. 2d 604 (1993). Under the federal law exclusively governing this industry, brokers **are not** motor carriers [moving companies]. The legal and contractual role of a broker and/or shipper's agent is to negotiate, arrange, or coordinate the interstate transportation. See 49 USC § 13102(2); see also 49 CFR § 371.2(a).

As a broker's role in the interstate transportation is limited; so too is their liability. A properly licensed broker is generally not liable for the acts, omissions or negligence of the moving company.

---

[16] See 49 CFR § 375.505(a) …The bill of lading must contain the terms and conditions of the contract…

Moreover, interstate brokers are generally not liable for the value of the goods involved in the interstate commerce. See *Professional Communs., Ins. v. Contract Freighters, Inc.*, 1741 F. Supp. 2d 546, 550 (D. Md. 2001) (citing commercial *Unions Ins. Co. v. Forward Air, Inc.*, 50 F. Supp. 2d 255, 257-59 (S.D.N.Y. 1999), and *Phoenix Assurance Co. v. Kmart Corp.*, 977 F. Supp. 319, 325-26 (D.N.J. 1997)).

For what acts or omissions are interstate brokers held liable?

Although interstate brokers may not generally be held liable for the acts or omissions of motor carriers; they can and are held accountable for breach of their duties to the consumer shipper as a broker. Additionally, interstate brokers can be civilly penalized and criminally prosecuted for failing to comply with the governing federal regulations.

As the consumer shipper's agent, interstate brokers have a legal duty to consumer shippers to act in good faith and issue honest and accurate estimates. Interstate brokers can and are held civilly and criminally liable for:

(1) Failing to clearly describe and represent their services as an interstate broker.[17]
(2) Failing to obtain an interstate license prior to conducting business.[18]
(3) Failing to secure and file a $75,000 surety bond with the FMCSA.
(4) Brokering a shipment to an unlicensed motor carrier.[19]
(5) Failing to provide potential consumer shippers with a complete listing of all motor carriers in the broker network.[20]
(6) Failing to provide consumer shippers with the booklet "Rights and Responsibilities when you Move."[21]

---

[17] See 49 CFR §§ 371.7; 371.107; 371.109(b)
[18] See 49 USC § 14901(d)(3)
[19] See 49 CFR § 371.105
[20] See 49 CFR § 371.109(a)
[21] See 49 CFR § 371.111

(7) Failing to provide a written estimate for services based upon the motor carrier's published tariff.[22]
(8) Failing to maintain a "master list" of brokered transactions.[23]
(9) Failing to have a properly signed "409" agreement with each licensed motor carrier in the network.[24]
(10) Failing to provide consumer shippers with written notice of deposit, refund, and cancellation policies. [25]
(11) Conducting business evidencing a pattern of fraudulent estimates – "lowballing"[26]

How can interstate brokers comply with the governing regulations, limit their liability, and protect consumers?

Interstate brokers must always operate in full compliance with the governing federal regulations. As a matter of policy and in practice, interstate brokers must maintain an ongoing commitment to customer service by providing full disclosure of role as a broker, honest and accurate estimates, and consumer advocacy and education. Additionally, interstate brokers must operate in accordance with internal policies which govern operations and include:

(1) Full disclosure of broker role and benefits to consumers

(2) Vetting of motor carriers prior to network affiliation

(3) Ongoing regulatory compliance monitoring of carriers

(4) Advocacy on behalf of consumer shippers - before, during, and after the move

(5) Ongoing training and legal compliance reviews

---

[22] See 49 CFR § 371.113 *et al.*
[23] See 49 CFR § 371.3 *et al.*
[24] See 49 CFR § 371.115; and § 375.409
[25] See 49 CFR § 371.117
[26] See 18 USC §§ 371; 1343; 1951; 1956(h); 1956(a)(1(A)(1)

Online Lead Providers

CHAPTER 20

The role of the Internet and online lead providers.

Consumers should be aware of the existence of Internet lead generator companies and how they differ from a regulated moving company. An Internet lead generator is a company that allows a consumer to enter their contact information and description of their upcoming move on the company's website. This service is typically provided free of charge. The Internet lead generator company then takes the consumer contact information and sells the data to several different moving companies. Each moving company that purchased the consumer contact information would call or e-mail the customer directly and attempt to sell their services.

Internet lead generator companies potentially offer a valuable service to consumers; assuming that the consumer is clearly informed that the website belongs to a lead generator company and not an actual moving company. Problems may arise if the consumer is under the misperception that the website belongs to an actual moving company. If a consumer wants to enter their contact information once and then receive several calls from competing moving companies, then an Internet lead generator company is a good choice. However, consumers should be aware that Internet lead generator companies are not regulated by the US DOT and generally make no representations, guarantees, or warrantees as to the quality of the moving companies calling to bid on the interstate move.

Advertising Regulations

CHAPTER 21

Are your website and advertisements legal?

The FMCSA has increased enforcement, violations and fines for interstate household goods moving companies in recent months. Strict enforcement has resulted in large fines to moving companies and owners of moving companies personally. One such area where moving companies may be vulnerable to large fines is in the content of their website and advertisements.

Large fines have recently been given for having misleading or wrong information on moving company websites. For example, fines have been issued for having photos of buildings, trucks, or storage facilities on the website that are not actually used by the moving company. The FMCSA has considered this practice to be false, misleading, and/or deceptive.

Legal requirements for advertisements and websites.

Federal law, under 49 CFR § 375.207(a) requires that moving companies publish "truthful, straightforward, and honest advertisements." A moving company can be held legally responsible for the content of their own advertisements/websites as well as the content of their agent's website such as lead provider websites where their name is listed.

The following are examples of advertising violations subject to financial penalty:
1. Not including your US DOT and ICC/MC numbers on all advertisements.
2. Using photos of buildings, trucks or storage units which you do not actually use.
3. Claiming to be members of an organization (e.g. BBB or AMSA) when you are not.
4. Having false letters of reference.
5. Claiming or implying to have a fleet of tractor trailers when you actually do not.
6. Claiming to be "licensed and bonded" when you are not actually "bonded."
7. Claiming to perform international moves when you only use a freight forwarder and you do not have your own OTI or NVOCC license from the Federal Marine Commission (*see* 46 CFR § 515.3).

Customer Service

CHAPTER 22

A successfully moving company fully complies with all governing regulations and provides top quality customer service. Good customer service is one of the most important aspects within a successful business. Quality service is defined by not only meeting the customer's needs but the ability to go above and beyond the customer's expectations. This ability to surpass expectations allows the customer to recognize the excellent organizational skills of your business and the commitment toward continually identifying individual customer needs. It is important to keep in mind that your business is judged not only by the service you perform, but also your customer communication throughout. The following is a general guideline for developing quality customer service.

First impressions.

The way a customer is greeted directly reflects upon the quality of your business. A professional greeting provides a positive reflection on the company. This can be accomplished by:

1. Directly stating the full company name followed by the employee's name. Example: "Moving Incorporated. This is Jane speaking" or

2. Stating gratitude for the company and addressing assistance. Example: "Thank you for calling Moving Incorporated. This is Jane, how can I help you?"

While the first example can be used as a greeting for general incoming calls, the second is a more personal greeting that can be used for direct lines toward inquires or complaints. The use of either of the two reflects the professionalism of the company and the services provided. A friendly greeting can provide an agitated, curious, or inquiring customer with a sense of security that any problems or questions they have can be solved.

Keeping Promises

Many times an agreement made between a company and the customer can be misinterpreted or broken. Never make promises to a customer that cannot be kept or give unrealistic or unclear estimations. Remember that the customer is relying on the company to reach deadlines. Always be clear and concise on what the exact agreement is and certain that the customer understands what is being said. This can be accomplished by:

1. Providing accurate estimates. Example: when giving an estimated pickup or delivery date range be consistent and concise. Instead of giving the customer a five day opening provide a more accurate time frame such as a two day estimation. The more precise the estimate the better. It is always advised that in-person visual estimates will be provided to customers.

2. Providing detailed information. Example: if a consumer shipper is inquiring about pricing give a detailed list of the services provided along with the cost. People like to know up front what to expect. Allow the consumer shipper to decide which service best suits their needs by explaining in detail what they will be receiving.

3. Providing honest answers. Example: honesty is the best policy. If you are unable to give an accurate answer, inform the customer that you do not have the information at this time. However do make sure that the consumer shipper's question is answered as soon as possible. A moving company must understand that consumer shippers are relying on the information and estimates provided to be honest and reasonably accurate.

4. Providing a mutual understanding. Example: if the consumer shipper does not understand the estimate, repeat in detail the full arrangement and follow up by repeating any aspect still not understood. Even when a consumer shipper appears to have a clear understanding, have them repeat back the agreement made to make sure there are no misinterpretations. A consumer shipper should always be informed well in advance of the move date of any and all possible charges over the estimate.

The customer is always right.

Even when taking the necessary steps to assure customer satisfaction mistakes occur. Whether it is a mistake made by the customer or the company the best way to turn a negative situation into a positive is to not only correct the problem, but to exceed the customer's expectations. Be polite and apologize for the misunderstanding and any inconvenience the situation may have caused. This can be accomplished by:

Being helpful and apologetic. Example: "I apologize for the inconvenience this has caused you, Mr. Smith. Please understand that we are doing everything we can at this time to correct the situation."

In some circumstances, delays and misunderstandings can create a sense of frustration for the customer. In these situations remember that it is the company's job to ensure customer satisfaction. Be sure to listen carefully and identify the customer's needs and/or complaints so the situation can be resolved as quickly as possible to avoid any further problems. Learn from the experience and apply it to other customers that may have the same or be experiencing similar problems.

Customer appreciation.

This part of customer service is often the most overlooked. Thanking your customers for choosing to do business with you is the finishing touch to assuring a positive experience.

This is especially important when dealing with customer complaints or unexpected situations that may arise that can cause complications. A show of appreciation can create a satisfied customer and can often become an important marketing tool.

A positive experience begins with a professional first impression and ends with an acknowledgment of appreciation. Surpassing expectations shows the customer the company's commitment toward creating a positive and satisfying experience.

Going above and beyond.

Taking that extra step to ensure the customer's needs are not only met but exceeded upon can make all the difference in getting a satisfied customer. Though the customer may not verbally acknowledge the steps your company has taken towards satisfaction, be assured that any extra efforts made do not go unnoticed. A satisfied customer will often return to a company they have had a previous positive experience with and share that experience with others, building up a positive reputation for the services provided. Even the smallest action reflects upon the company. Examine the services the company provides and think of ways to continually improve upon them. Ask yourself:

- What can be done to improve customer satisfaction?

- Has the customer's needs been met and/or exceeded?

- How has the company differentiated itself from others offering similar services?

- Has the customer felt like their satisfaction is the number one priority?

Taking these extra steps to assure a positive experience for each customer is an important step toward maintaining a satisfied customer.

FMCSA Investigations

CHAPTER 23

About the Federal Motor Carrier Safety Administration.

The Federal Motor Carrier Safety Administration (FMCSA) is a subset of the United States Department of Transportation. It is the chief regulatory enforcement agency governing interstate household goods carriers and brokers. This agency, established in January 1, 2000, is dedicated to increasing the safety of interstate commercial motor vehicles and saving lives by reducing injury and fatalities of crashes. The FMCSA oversees, regulates, and educates interstate commercial moving companies engaged in the transportation of commercial goods, hazardous materials, and consumer household goods.

The FMCSA's regulation of household goods moving companies involves the licensing of carriers, consumer education and protection, and investigating violations and taking enforcement actions. Since 2005, the FMCSA has taken the lead role in promoting consumer education and taking enforcement actions against moving companies operating out of compliance with the governing federal regulations.

In regard to moving companies, their interaction with the FMCSA generally takes the form of an investigative review or audit. These investigative reviews have become more commonplace over the last few years and have been a helpful tool ensuring that moving companies are operating in accordance with safety and consumer protection regulations. However, in cases where a moving company is not prepared for an investigative review the legal consequences and financial penalties may be significant.

Generally, what types of investigative reviews and audits are performed?

The FMCSA investigators legally may visit a moving company and conduct a review at any time for any reason with little or no notice. There are generally three types of investigative reviews or audits which are performed: (1) new entrant audits, (2) safety reviews, and (3) economic or legal compliance reviews. Each investigative review or audit has a different purpose with different consequences for non-compliance.

(1) New entrant audits are generally conducted for every moving company within the first 90 days of becoming active. These audits are primarily educational in nature and designed to ensure that the new entrant moving company has a basic understanding of the safety and economic regulations. New entrant audits do not generally result in any fine or violation being assessed against the moving company.

In practice, the new entrant audits are not in depth training sessions. In some areas the new entrant audits are conducted by subcontracted state employees and not fully trained FMCSA investigators. A moving company should not rely on the FMCSA to provide a complete educational training session. Always remember that the FMCSA is primarily an enforcement agency. It is rightly assumed by the FMCSA that when a moving company obtains a license to operate it understands and will comply with all the governing regulations.

(2) Safety reviews are focused on a moving company's compliance with safety and operations regulations such as vehicle operations, driver's hours of service and log books, driver's files, record retention, vehicle maintenance, drug and alcohol programs, and licensing and insurance. The safety review is perhaps the most important review conducted by FMCSA investigators. In short, safety reviews save lives. The safety regulations are designed to ensure that the interstate roadways are safe. A moving company must ensure that it understands and stays in compliance with all the safety regulations.

A FMCSA investigator conducting a safety investigation will generally review driver hours of service logs books, vehicle maintenance records, and a moving company's compliance with the mandatory drug and alcohol program. Depending on the type of violations discovered a moving company could face financial penalty, be placed temporarily or permanently out of service, and possibly face criminal penalty.

(3) Economic or legal compliance reviews generally focus on a moving company's compliance with the consumer protection regulations. FMCSA investigators conducting an economic or legal compliance review will inspect the carrier's tariff and shipping documents including the bill of lading, orders for service, estimates, and inventory logs. The FMCSA investigator has the task of making certain that the consumer shipper was charged rates in accordance with the properly published tariff and that the carrier's interactions with the consumer shipper were in full compliance with the regulations. Depending on the types of violations discovered the moving company could face financial penalty or criminal charges.

The FMCSA investigator may conduct both a safety review and an economic or legal compliance review at the same time. The length of time the investigator spends at the moving company's facility depends on the quantity of business conducted and the intent of the investigation. Generally, investigations take anywhere from one day to a few days to a couple weeks in extreme cases. The familiarity and expertise of the individual investigator generally will determine the focus of the review.

What may trigger an audit/investigation?

As discussed above, new entrant audits are generally conducted for all new carriers within the first 90 days of activation. Safety reviews and economic or legal compliance reviews can be triggered in a variety of different manners. Reviews have been conducted randomly by the FMCSA's household goods task force where they will target a particular metropolitan area and perform spot inspections on as many moving companies as possible in a fixed period of time. More commonly, safety reviews are triggered by excessive roadside safety violations. Economic or legal compliance reviews are normally triggered by high numbers of consumer complaints.

Is the FMCSA required to give a moving company any notice before a review?

Operating with interstate moving company authority is a privilege and not a right. As such, the FMCSA may conduct investigative reviews at any time for any reason with or without notice. It is assumed by the FMCSA that any licensed moving company understands and is operating in compliance with governing federal regulations, and therefore an investigative review should not be a burden.

What information must be disclosed to the FMCSA investigator?

The investigative powers of the FMCSA are broad. Federal law provides authority for the FMCSA as an agency of the Unites States Department of Transportation to inspect the land, buildings, and equipment of a moving company or broker. Moreover, under 49 U.S.C. section 14122(b)(2) the FMCSA may inspect and copy ***"any record"*** of the moving company or broker deemed to have any relevance to its investigation. This federal code is written so broadly that it may include all shipping contracts, corporate records, financial documents, or any other records or document of the moving company.

How to prepare before the FMCSA review.

The best way to prepare for an investigative review is to have a full understanding and operate in compliance with all of the safety, economic, and consumer protection regulations governing the industry. An internal program of training and re-training is essential to stay current with the frequently changing regulations.

If a moving company is provided with notice of an impending investigative review there are specific steps that can be taken to help the review go as smooth as possible. First and foremost, cooperate with the FMCSA investigator. Keep in mind that, although their role is regulatory enforcement, the FMCSA investigators are not the enemy. Most FMCSA investigators have the same goals as the moving companies to operate in compliance with the governing regulations. An FMCSA investigative review should not generally be seen as confrontational.

Although cooperation is essential, a moving company should understand that it has legal rights during the investigation. Since all reviews have the potential of resulting in financial penalty or in rare cases, criminal charges, it is advised that legal counsel is always consulted prior to making any statements to the FMCSA investigator. As a general rule, a moving company should never sign any written statement prepared by the FMCSA investigator without independent legal counsel's review. Any oral statement made or written statement signed can and will be taken as an admission of guilt for any violations charged by the FMCSA investigator.

What to do during a FMCSA investigative review.

In most cases the FMCSA may only review records for a time period of one year prior to the review. It is best to provide the FMCSA investigator with all the documents requested in an organized fashion. The easier it is for the investigator to find the information they need the quicker the investigation will be completed.

Generally, investigative reviews are not interactive. They usually consist of the FMCSA investigator going through the various records and files. It is best to provide the FMCSA investigator with a comfortable and quiet place to review the documents.

Once the FMCSA investigator has finished reviewing and copying the documents he or she will prepare a summary of the findings and review them with the moving company. The investigator should take as much time as necessary to review, in detail, each and every finding. However, in practice this review is sometimes rushed through.

After the investigator has reviewed the findings with the moving company he or she will ask a company representative to sign the review. Much like a traffic ticket, the signature on the review findings document is not an admission of guilt or liability. However, many FMCSA investigators have a standard practice of including with the review document a "statement" which IS AN ADMISSION OF GUILT IF SIGNED. It is often difficult to tell the difference between the documents. Therefore, it is advised that the moving company respectfully decline to sign any documents without having them first reviewed by legal counsel.

What to do after an FMCSA investigative review.

If a moving company is operating in compliance with the regulations then the investigative review will result in no action taken against them. However, in the event a violation is discovered different actions may be taken.

When a safety review is conducted the findings of the review will usually resulting in the ranking of the moving company's safety compliance as: (1) satisfactory, (2) conditional, or (3) unsatisfactory. A satisfactory ranking is what all moving companies should strive for. This ranking demonstrates that the moving company is operating in compliance with the safety regulations and has a satisfactory safety record.

A conditional ranking demonstrates that the moving company needs to improve its safety fitness level. A moving company with a conditional ranking must work to improve its operations to ensure compliance with the regulations. After appropriate steps have been taken to improve its operations the moving company should invite the FMCSA back to conduct a follow up review. If all steps have been taken to improve its operational fitness the moving company's raking should be increased to satisfactory.

An unsatisfactory ranking is the most serious of the three rankings. It means that the moving company is not operating in compliance with the safety regulations and is likely a danger to the public. An unsatisfactory ranking generally results in the moving company being placed out of service. A moving company with an unsatisfactory ranking and placed out of service may not operate and must take immediate and substantive actions to correct the violations. Only after evidence or substantial corrective actions have been submitted to the FMCSA will a carrier's ranking be increased to conditional and then to satisfactory.

An economic or legal compliance review will result in no action being taken against the carrier if no violations are discovered. However, where violations are discovered the FMCSA will generally issue a charging document called a Notice of Claim. The Notice of Claim is a legal document which sets out the violations discovered and assesses a civil penalty for each. Violations can range from $1,000 to hundreds of thousands of dollars depending on the charges. Any carrier receiving a Notice of Claim should retain legal counsel as soon as possible.

FMCSA Enforcement Actions:

Year	Total fines nationwide	Largest fine against an individual moving company
2006	$16,888,990.00	$37,390.00
2007	$24,348,668.00	$98,000.00
2008	$25,423,390.00	$38,800.00
2009	$27,847,730.00	$47,500.00
2010	$28,090,842.00	$281,100.00
2011	$28,275,406.00	$184,100.00
2012	$31,814,508.00	$34,340.00

Source as March 2014:
http://www.fmcsa.dot.gov/facts-research/enforcement-reports/enforcement-reports.aspx

Independent Contractors

CHAPTER 24

Properly classifying a worker's employment status as either an employee or an independent contractor (IC) is a critical and complicated process. While labeling a worker an IC can provide businesses with significant benefits, misclassification of the worker can lead to significant fines and penalties.

No single rule or test distinguishes whether a worker is an employee or an IC, thus the classification between the two types of workers is often confusing. Decisions on whether a worker is an employee or an IC must be made on a case-by-case basis. Since each state uses a different test in determining whether a worker is an employee or an IC, it is important for an employer to check with their local state labor board for classification details. The charts to follow are designed to help an employer understand:

1. The differences between a W-2 employee and an IC;
2. The benefits and consequences of hiring ICs;
3. Tests used to determine whether a worker is an employee or IC;
4. Factors to consider when choosing between an employee and an IC;
5. Steps an employer can take to prevent misclassification.

The chart below defines the key difference between a worker who is an "employee" and one who is an "independent contractor":

Employee	Independent Contractor
• Must have employer-employee relationship. • An employer-employee relationship exists when a person who hires an individual to perform services has the right to exercise control over the manner and means by which the individual performs his/her services.	• Independent contractors are people who contract to perform services for others, but do not have the legal status of employees. • Employer's right to exercise control is limited to accepting and rejecting the final results.

What is an independent contractor?

Independent contractors, or ICs, are people who contract to perform services for others, but do not have the legal status of employees. Because many employment laws and tax rules that cover employees do not apply to ICs, businesses can save time, money, and headaches by hiring ICs instead of employees.

What are the benefits and consequences of hiring ICs?

Benefits	Consequences
• **Savings.** Usually, money is saved by hiring ICs because employers do not have to pay: Salaries, Federal payroll taxes, State unemployment insurance premiums, Employee benefits, and Office space and equipment. • **Less Lawsuits.** Reduced types of lawsuits such as job discrimination or wrongful termination. • **Flexibility.** For example, you can pay an IC to accomplish only a specific task, allowing your business to get specialized expertise for s short period. • **No Laying Off or Firing.** Once the IC's job is finished, the relationship is over.	• **Significant Penalties for Misclassification.** If business misclassifies employee as an IC, business must pay the IRS all back taxes owed, with interest, plus a penalty of 12% to 35% of the tax bill. • **Frequent Audits.** Audits by state agencies are even more common than IRS audits. An investigation by your state unemployment compensation agency will ensue, and you will be subject to fines and penalties if it determines that workers whom you classified as ICs should have been classified as employees for unemployment compensation purpose

How does the government determine whether a worker is an employee or independent contractor?

Most people who qualify as ICs follow their own trade, business, or profession – that is they are in business for themselves. They earn their livelihoods from their own independent businesses instead of depending on their employer. However, a worker does not have to be a professional to be an IC. A person you hire to paint your office or mow your lawn can be in business for himself or herself and qualify as an IC. For example, the IRS and the California Employment Development Department (EDD) employ different tests to determine whether a worker is an employee or IC. The chart below lists each test:

IRS	California EDD
1. Can earn a profit or suffer a loss from the activity	1. Worker is instructed or supervised by employer while he or she is working
2. Furnishes the tools and materials needed to do the job	2. Worker can quit or be discharged at any time
3. Is paid by the job	3. Work performed is part of your regular business
4. Works for more than one client company at a time	4. Worker has a separately established business
5. Invests in equipment and facilities	5. Worker free to make business decisions which affect his or her ability to profit from the work
6. Pays his or her own business and traveling expenses	6. Individual has a substantial investment which would subject him or her to a financial risk of loss
7. Hires and pays assistants, and	7. Employer has employees who do the same type of work
8. Sets his or her own working hours.	8. Worker furnishes the tools, equipment, or supplies used to perform the work
	9. Work is considered unskilled or semi-skilled labor
	10. Worker paid a fixed salary, an hourly wage, or based on a piece rate basis
	11. Worker previously perform the same or similar services for you as an employee
	12. Worker believes that he or she is an employee

In choosing which route to take, there are several factors worth considering. The chart below describes the various factors:

	IC	Employee
Tax Obligations	• You're not required to withhold taxes from the amount you pay the worker, and you don't have to pay any portion of the worker's Social Security and Medicare taxes. • Only tax responsibility is to complete a Form 1099-MISC at the end of the year if you paid the IC $600 or more during the year.	• You must make an employer's contribution for the worker's Social security and Medicare Taxes. • You are also responsible for withholding federal and state income taxes and the worker's share of Social Security and Medicare taxes, and for keeping records and reporting on these items to the federal government. • You must send the employee a Form W-2.
Workers' Compensation	• Generally, does not pay for workers' compensation for an IC.	• You must carry workers' compensation insurance for the employee.
Unemployment Compensation	• Generally, an employer does not make contributions to a state unemployment fund or pay the federal unemployment tax for an IC.	• You must contribute to an unemployment insurance fund in your state and pay a federal unemployment tax.

	IC	Employee
Job Benefits	• Paid only for time spent working – and are responsible for paying for their own health insurance and retirement savings plan.	• An employer usually provides job benefits for an employee, such as paid vacations, sick leave and holidays, health insurance and retirement plan.
Workspace	• Usually, but not always, pays for workspace and equipment.	• Employer provides workspace and equipment for an employee.
Firing the Worker	• Hired for a set assignment to be completed by a fixed deadline. • If IC isn't satisfactory, you can simply turn to another IC for future work.	• If you become unhappy with an employee's work and he or she doesn't improve, you will likely have to fire the worker – often a traumatic and legally hazardous course of action.
Cost	• Hourly rate of an IC may be relatively high because the worker must earn enough to cover business expenses and taxes.	• Hourly rate you pay an employee may be relatively low – but true costs also include money you pay for taxes, insurance, job benefits, workspace, and equipment.

	IC	Employee
Government Regulations	• Subject to fewer legal restrictions.	• Subject to a wide range of governmental regulations intended to protect employees.
Liability for Workers' Actions	• Employer generally not liable for negligence of that person.	• Employer legally liable for injuries or property damage caused by an employee's negligence.
Liability for Injury to Worker	• Can recover medical bills and lost income from your business, as well as money for pain and suffering. • IC must show that employer was negligent first before damages can be collected.	• Employer is responsible for medical treatment for an employee hurt on the job and for paying money to partially cover the employee's lost wages.
Worker's Preference	• Greater control over working hours and conditions and to maintain the freedom to work for several businesses.	• May prefer to be an employee because status promises a steady, predictable salary and benefits.
Employer's Preference	• Allows more flexibility to adjust to fluctuating needs.	• Business has that worker's undivided loyalty and can better control the worker's hours and methods of doing the job.

Consumer Checklist

CHAPTER 25

When hiring a moving company:

- ☐ Get three written estimates before hiring an interstate moving company.
- ☐ Verify that the interstate moving company is properly licensed and insured. http://safer.fmcsa.dot.gov/CompanySnapshot.aspx
- ☐ Ask for references from the mover and call them to verify their accuracy.
- ☐ Read and understand all estimates and contracts before signing.
- ☐ Make certain to receive and read the booklet: "Your Rights and Responsibilities When You Move."
- ☐ Verify that the moving company has a neutral dispute resolution program.
- ☐ Understand that an estimate is only valid for the services and number of items to be moved as described in writing. If, on the day of the move you add additional items to be moved or require additional services your price will increase. Most estimates are not guaranteed.
- ☐ Have a clear understanding of the pick-up and delivery window. Understand that, in most cases, delivery is not a guaranteed date.
- ☐ Purchase full replacement value insurance to protect your property.
- ☐ Declare and insure all items of extraordinary value.

Questions a consumer should ask an estimator:

☐ Does the company have active US DOT and ICC/MC license numbers?

☐ Will the estimate be binding or non-binding?

☐ Will final charges be based upon weight or cubic feet?

☐ Will the company provide references from satisfied customers?

☐ What are the charges for packing services?

☐ What are the charges for "full coverage insurance," and what is covered?

☐ Which neutral arbitration program does the company participate in?

☐ Is the estimate provided in writing and does it list all services ordered?

☐ Does the company charge extra for stairs, long carry, shuttle, storage, appliance serving, etc?

☐ Are the pickup or delivery dates guaranteed?

☐ What form of payment is accepted at delivery?

☐ How long after delivery do I have to file a claim for damages?

On the day of the move a consumer should:

☐ Carefully read and understand all documents ***before*** signing. Estimates must be completed, approved by you, and signed ***before*** the moving company begins any work.

☐ Have all property professionally packed.

☐ Be present at the pickup, supervise the movers' work and stay until all packing and loading is finished.

☐ Accompany the movers as they inventory your household goods, and resolve any questions regarding the condition of materials being moved.

☐ Make sure to receive and keep copies of all the shipping documents until the goods are delivered, the charges are paid, and any claims are settled.

☐ Before the movers leave take one final look throughout the house to make certain nothing has been left behind.

On the delivery day a consumer should:

☐ Be prepared and available to supervise unloading and unpacking of your goods.

☐ According to federal law, pay the mover in the form of payment agreed upon as written on your contract before your goods are unloaded.

☐ Direct the movers on where to unload and place the items in your home.

☐ Inspect all property for damage or missing items and document damages in writing.

☐ Note on the inventory logs all boxes or other items that are damaged or missing.

After the move a consumer should:

☐ Finish unpacking and inspect all property for damage or missing items.

☐ File a claim with the mover for any damage or loss as quickly as possible after the delivery. Consumer shippers have nine months after delivery to submit claims. Send claim letters via certified mail.

☐ Work with the moving company customer service department to resolve any outstanding issues.

Appendix

CHAPTER 26

I. GLOSSARY

ACCESSORIAL SERVICES: These are services such as packing, appliance servicing, unpacking, or piano stair carries that a shipper may request to be performed. Charges for these services may be in addition to the line haul charges.

ACTUAL CASH VALUE (ACV): Money equal to the cost of replacing lost, stolen or damaged property after depreciation. A method of determining the worth of an improvement.

ADVANCED CHARGES: Charges for services not performed by the moving company but instead by a professional, craftsman or other third party at the shipper's request. The charges for these services are paid for by the moving company and added to your bill of lading charges.

AGENT: A local moving company authorized to act on behalf of the carrier.

APPLIANCE SERVICE: Preparation of major electrical appliances to make them safe for shipment.

BILL OF LADING: The receipt for the goods and the contract for their transportation.

BROKER: An interstate broker is any person or company who for compensation arranged for or offers to arrange the transportation of property by an authorized moving company.

BULKY ARTICLE: Include such items as boats, snowmobiles, golf carts, and campers. These "bulky" items usually carry an extra charge to compensate the hauler for the difficulty of loading and unloading, as well as for their unusual bulk or low-weight density.

CERTIFIED SCALE: Any scale designed for weighing motor vehicles, including trailers or semi-trailers not attached to a tractor, and certified by an authorized scale inspection and licensing authority. A certified scale may also be a platform or warehouse type scale that is properly inspected and certified.

CARRIER/MOVER: The moving company and its agents, contractors, employees, and representatives.

CASH ON DELIVERY (COD): This means payment is required at the time of delivery and prior to unloading at the destination residence (or warehouse).

CLAIM: A statement of loss or damage to any of the household goods while in the custody of the moving company or its affiliated agent.

CONSULTANT: Person with whom a shipper discusses the particular move requirements, who usually makes a note of items to be moved, provides information about their company and an estimate for services.

COST PER CUBIC METER: A rate given on the estimated space that the property will fill on a truck / container.

COST PER 100 LBS.: A rate given on the estimated weight of the property being transported.

COST PER CUBIC FOOT: A rate given on the estimated space the property will fill on a truck / container.

COST PER HOUR: A rate given per hour based on the number of men and size of truck that will be charged on the time taken to carry out the move.

DEPARTMENT OF TRANSPORTATION (DOT): The federal agency which, through the Surface Transportation Board within the DOT, governs the interstate transportation industry, including movers of household goods.

ESTIMATE, BINDING: An agreement made in advance with the moving company. It provides that the total cost of the move will be based upon the quantities (specific item list) and services shown on the estimate.

ESTIMATE, NON-BINDING: What the moving company believes the cost will be, based upon the estimated weight of the shipment and the accessorial services requested. A non-binding estimate is not binding on the mover. The final charges will be based upon the actual weight of the shipment, the services provided, and the tariff provisions in effect.

GUARANTEED PICKUP AND DELIVERY SERVICE: An additional level of service featuring guaranteed dates of service. The moving company will provide reimbursement for any delays. This premium service is often subject to minimum weight requirements.

HIGH VALUE ARTICLE: Items included in a shipment that are valued at more than $100 per pound. These items should be disclosed to the moving company to ensure they are protected accordingly.

INTRASTATE: Intrastate transportation of household goods is the movement of property from an origin to a destination within the same state. For example, when a shipper moves from Dallas, Texas, to Austin, Texas. Moving companies performing services as an intrastate mover must be licensed with that individual state's regulatory body. Generally, the regulatory agencies governing intrastate moving companies are the States' Public Utilities Commission (PUC) or Department of Transportation (State DOT).

INTERNATIONAL: International transportation of household goods is the movement of property from an origin in one country to a destination in another country. For example, when a shipper moves from the United States to England. For Unites States based companies, international moves are regulated by the Federal Maritime Commission. (www.fmc.gov).

INTERSTATE: Interstate transportation of household goods is the movement of property from an origin in one state to a destination in another state. For example, when a shipper moves from San Francisco, California to Phoenix, Arizona. Interstate moving companies transporting household goods are regulated and licensed by the U.S. Department of Transportation Federal Motor Carrier Safety Administration. (FMCSA) More information about the regulatory and licensing requirements may be found at www.fmcsa.dot.gov.

INVENTORY: The detailed descriptive list of the household goods showing the number and condition of each item.

LINE HAUL CHARGES: The charges for the vehicle transportation portion of the move. These charges, if separately stated, apply in addition to the special/additional service charges.

LONG CARRY: A charge for carrying articles excessive distances between the mover's vehicle and your residence. Charges for these services may be in addition to the line haul charges.

OPERATING AUTHORITY: The certification issued by a state or federal governmental department authorizing a mover or carrier to move household goods between designated geographical areas.

ORDER FOR SERVICE: The document authorizing the motor carrier to transport the household goods. An order for services is not a contract.

ORDER (BILL OF LADING) NUMBER: The number used to identify and track the shipment.

PBO (packed by owner): Occurs when articles are packed by the shipper, for moving.

PEAK SEASON RATES: Higher line haul charges that are applicable during the summer months.

SHIPPER: The customer or customer's agent or representative who engaged the carrier to perform interstate domestic moving services.

SHUTTLE SERVICE: The use of a smaller vehicle to provide service to residences not accessible to the mover's normal line haul vehicles.

SPECIAL/ADDITIONAL SERVICES: These are services such as packing, appliance servicing, unpacking, or piano stair carries that the shipper request to be performed (or that are necessary because of landlord requirements or other special circumstances). Charges for these services may be in addition to the line haul charges.

STAIRS FLIGHT CHARGE: A charge for carrying items up or down flights of stairs. Charges for these services may be in addition to the line haul charges.

STORAGE IN TRANSIT (SIT): Temporary warehouse storage of the shipment pending further transportation. For example, if the shipper's new home isn't quite ready to occupy they might request SIT.

STORAGE VAULTS: Large wooden container, in which the property is loaded into, sealed and then stacked away.

TARIFF: An issuance (in whole or in part) containing rates, rules, regulations, classifications, or other provisions. The Surface Transportation Board requires that a tariff contain three specific items. First, an accurate description of the services the mover offers to the public. Second, the specific applicable rates (or the basis for calculating the specific applicable rates) and service terms for services offered to the public. Third, the mover's tariff must be arranged in a way that allows you to determine the exact rate(s) and service terms applicable to your shipment.

VALUATION: The degree of worth of the shipment. The valuation charge compensates the mover for assuming a greater degree of liability than is provided for in its base transportation charges.

WAREHOUSE HANDLING: An additional charge applicable each time storage-in-transit service is provided.

WEIGHT TICKET/CERTIFICATE: The truck is weighed before and after the shipment is loaded. Each time the truck is weighed, the driver gets a dated weight ticket listing the weight and where the truck was weighed. A copy of the weight ticket should be with the freight bill.

Headquarters:

Federal Motor Carrier Safety Administration
1200 New Jersey Avenue, SE
Suite W60-300,
Washington, DC 20590

Main Information Line:	1-800-832-5660
Administration:	202-366-8773
Chief Counsel:	202-493-0349
Civil Rights:	202-366-8810
Communications:	202-366-9999
Enforcement and Program Delivery:	202-366-2525
Regulatory Ombudsman:	202-366-0596
Policy and Program Development:	202-366-8773
Research and Information:	202-366-2525

Service Centers:

Eastern Service Center
802 Cromwell Park Drive, Suite N
Glen Burnie, MD 21061
Phone: (443) 703-2240
Fax: (443) 703-2253
Territories covered: CT, DC, DE, MA, MD, ME, NJ, NH, NY, PA, PR, RI, VA, VT, WV

Midwestern Service Center
19900 Governors Drive, Suite 210
Olympia Fields, IL 60461
Phone: (708) 283-3577
Fax: (708) 283-3579
Territories covered: IA, IL, IN, KS, MI, MO, MN, NE, OH, WI

Southern Service Center
1800 Century Boulevard, NE
Suite 1700
Atlanta, GA 30345-3220
Phone: (404) 327-7400
Fax: (404) 327-7349
Territories covered: AL, AR, FL, GA, KY, LA, MS, NC, NM, OK, SC, TN, TX

Western Service Center
Golden Hills Office Centre
12600 West Colfax Avenue
Suite B-300
Lakewood, CO 80215
Phone: (303) 407-2350
Fax: (303) 407-2339
Territories covered: American Samoa, AK, AZ, CA, CO, Guam, HI, ID, Mariana Islands, MT, ND, NV, OR, SD, UT, WA, WY

Field Offices Location Address:

Alabama Division
500 Eastern Boulevard, Suite 200
Montgomery, AL 36117
Phone: (334) 223-7244
Fax: (334) 223-7700

Alaska Division
Frontier Building, Suite 260
3601 C Street
Anchorage, AK 99503
Phone: (907) 271-4068
Fax: (907) 271-4069

Arizona Division
One Arizona Center
400 East Van Buren Street, Suite 401
Phoenix, AZ 85004-2223
Phone: (602) 379-6851
Fax: (602) 379-3627

Arkansas Division 2527
Federal Building
700 W. Capitol Avenue
Little Rock, AR 72201
Phone: (501) 324-5050
Fax: (501) 324-6562

California Division
1325 J Street, Suite 1540
Sacramento, CA 95814
Phone: (916) 930-2760
Fax: (916) 930-2778

Colorado Division
12300 West Dakota Avenue, Suite 130
Lakewood, CO 80228
Phone: (720) 963-3130
Fax: (720) 963-3131

Connecticut Division
628-2 Hebron Avenue, Suite 303
Glastonbury, CT 06033
Phone: (860) 659-6700
Fax: (860) 659-6725

Delaware Division
J. Allen Frear Federal Building
300 South New Street, Suite 1105
Dover, DE 19904-6726
Phone: (302) 734-8173
Fax: (302) 734-5380

District of Columbia Division
1990 K Street, NW, Suite 510
Washington, DC 20006
Phone: (202) 219-3553
Fax: (202) 219-3546

Florida Division
545 John Knox Road, Room 102
Tallahassee, FL 32303
Phone: (850) 942-9338
Fax: (850) 942-9680

Georgia Division
Two Crown Center
1745 Phoenix Boulevard, Suite 380
Atlanta, GA 30349
Phone: (678) 284-5130
Fax: (678) 284-5146

Hawaii Division
300 Ala Moana Boulevard, Room 3-243
Box 50226
Honolulu, HI 96850
Phone: (808) 541-2790
Fax: (808) 541-2702

Idaho Division
3200 North LakeHarbor Lane, Suite 161
Boise, ID 83703
Phone: (208) 334-1842
Fax: (208) 334-1046

Illinois Division
3250 Executive Park Drive
Springfield, IL 62703-4514
Phone: (217) 492-4608
Fax: (217) 492-4986

Indiana Division
575 North Pennsylvania Street, Room 261
Indianapolis, IN 46204
Phone: (317) 226-7474
Fax: (317) 226-5657

Iowa Division
105 6th Street
Ames, IA 50010-6337
Phone: (515) 233-7400
Fax: (515) 233-7494

Kansas Division
1303 SW First American Place, Suite 200
Topeka, KS 66604-4040
Phone: (785) 271-1260
Fax: (785) 228-9725

Kentucky Division
330 West Broadway, Room 124
Frankfort, KY 40601
Phone: (502) 223-6779
Fax: (502) 223-6767

Louisiana Division
5304 Flanders Drive, Suite A
Baton Rouge, LA 70808
Phone: (225) 757-7640
Fax: (225) 757-7636

Maine Division
Edmund S. Muskie Federal Building
40 Western Avenue, Room 608
Augusta, ME 04330
Phone: (207) 622-8358
Fax: (207) 622-8477

Maryland Division
City Crescent Building
10 South Howard Street, Suite 2710
Baltimore, MD 21201
Phone: (410) 962-2889
Fax: (410) 962-3916

Massachusetts Division
55 Broadway, Bldg 3, Room 1-35
Cambridge, MA 02142
Phone: (617) 494-2770
Fax: (617) 494-2783

Michigan Division
315 West Allegan, Room 219
Lansing, MI 48933
Phone: (517) 853-5990
Fax: (517) 377-1868

Minnesota Division
380 Jackson Street
Galtier Plaza, Suite 500
St. Paul, MN 55101
Phone: (651) 291-6150
Fax: (651) 291-6001

Mississippi Division
666 North Street, Suite 103
Jackson, MS 39202-3199
Phone: (601) 965-4219
Fax: (601) 965-4674

Missouri Division
3219 Emerald Lane, Suite 500
Jefferson City, MO 65109
Phone: (573) 636-3246
Fax: (573) 636-8901

Montana Division
2880 Skyway Drive
Helena, MT 59602
Phone: (406) 449-5304
Fax: (406) 449-5318

Nebraska Division
100 Centennial Mall North,
Room 406 Lincoln, NE 68508
Phone 402-437-5986
Fax - 402 -437-5837

Nevada Division
705 North Plaza Street, Suite 204
Carson City, NV 89701
Phone: (775) 687-5335
Fax: (775) 687-8353

New Hampshire Division
70 Commercial Street, Suite 102
Concord, NH 03301
Phone: (603) 228-3112
Fax: (603) 223-0390

New Jersey Division
840 Bear Tavern Road, Suite 310
West Trenton, NJ 08628
Phone: (609) 637-4222
Fax: (609) 538-4913

New Mexico Division
2400 Louisiana Blvd. NE
Suite 520 AFC-5
Albuquerque, NM 87110
Phone: (505) 346-7858
Fax: (505) 346-7859

New York Division
Leo W. O'Brien Federal Building
Room 719
Clinton Avenue & North Pearl Street
Albany, NY 12207
Phone: (518) 431-4145
Fax: (518) 431-4140

North Carolina Division
310 New Bern Avenue, Suite 468
Raleigh, NC 27601
Phone: (919) 856-4378
Fax: (919) 856-4369

North Dakota Division
1471 Interstate Loop
Bismarck, ND 58503
Phone: (701) 250-4346
Fax: (701) 250-4389

Ohio Division
200 North High Street, Room 328
Columbus, OH 43215
Phone: (614) 280-5657
Fax: (614) 280-6875

Oklahoma Division
300 North Meridian, Suite 106 South
Oklahoma City, OK 73107
Phone: (405) 605-6047
Fax: (405) 605-6176

Oregon Division
The Equitable Center
530 Center Street, NE
Suite 100
Salem, OR 97301-3740
Phone: (503) 399-5775
Fax: (503) 399-5838

Pennsylvania Division
228 Walnut Street, Room 560
Harrisburg, PA 17101
Phone: (717) 221-4443
Fax: (717) 221-4552

Puerto Rico Division
Torre Chardón
350 Chardón Street Suite 207
Hato Rey, PR 00918
Phone: (787) 766-5985
Fax: (787) 766-5015

Rhode Island Division
20 Risho Avenue, Suite E
East Providence, RI 02914
Phone: (401) 431-6010
Fax: (401) 431-6019

South Carolina Division
1835 Assembly Street, Suite 1253
Columbia, SC 29201-2430
Phone: (803) 765-5414
Fax: (803) 765-5413

South Dakota Division
116 East Dakota Avenue, Suite B
Pierre, SD 57501
Phone: (605) 224-8202
Fax: (605) 224-1766

Tennessee Division
640 Grassmere Park, Suite 111
Nashville, TN 37211
Phone: (615) 781-5781
Fax: (615) 781-5755

Texas Division
826 Federal Building
300 East 8th Street, Room 865
Austin, TX 78701
Phone: (512) 536-5980
Fax: (512) 916-5980

Utah Division
2520 West 4700 South, Suite 9B
Salt Lake City, UT 84118-1847
Phone: (801) 963-0096
Fax: (801) 963-0086

Vermont Division
FMCSA - Vermont Division
P.O. Box 338
87 State Street,
Room 305 Montpelier, VT 05601
Tel. (802) 828-4480
Fax (802) 828-4581

Virginia Division
400 North 8th Street, Suite 780
Richmond, VA 23219-4827
Phone: (804) 771-8585
Fax: (804) 771-8681

Washington Division
Evergreen Plaza Building
711 South Capitol Way, Suite 502
Olympia, WA 98501
Phone: (360) 753-9875
Fax: (360) 753-9024

West Virginia Division
700 Washington Street East
Geary Plaza, Suite 205
Charleston, WV 25301
Phone: (304) 347-5935
Fax: (304) 347-5617

Wisconsin Division
Highpoint Office Park
567 D'Onofrio Drive, Suite 101
Madison, WI 53719-2844
Phone: (608) 829-7530
Fax: (608) 829-7540

Wyoming Division
1637 Stillwater Avenue, Suite F
Cheyenne, WY 82009
Phone: (307) 772-2305
Fax: (307) 772-2905

III. MOVING AND STORAGE ASSOCIATIONS

Note: *All products, companies, associations, and/or organizations referenced in this book are included for informational purposes only and their inclusion in this book should not be understood to be their expressed or implied endorsement of the information contained within or the opinions of the author. The author does not endorse any company, association, or organization referenced in this legal guide.*

Household Goods Forwarders Association of America, Inc.
5904 Richmond Highway, Suite 404
Alexandria, VA 22303
Phone: (703) 317-9950
http://www.hhgfaa.org

Alaska Movers Association
3443 Minnesota Drive
Anchorage, AK 99503
Phone: (907) 276-1149
Fax: (907) 274-1946

California Moving & Storage Association
4281 Katella Avenue, Suite 205
Los Alamitos - California - 90720-6513
Phone: (714) 236-2060
http://www.thecmsa.org

Canadian Association of Movers
2085 Hurontario Street, Suite 525
Mississauga, Ontario, Canada L5A 4G1
Phone: (905) 848-6579
http://www.mover.net

Claims Prevention and Procedure Council
P.O. Box 1117
Newburgh, IN 47629-1117
Phone: 866-276-5656
http://www.claimsnet.org

Movers & Warehousemen's Association of Connecticut
60 Forest Street
Hartford, CT 06105
Phone: (860) 520-4455
Fax: (860) 520-4567

Florida Movers & Warehousemen's Association
PO Box 14629
Tallahassee, FL 32317
Phone: (850) 222-6000
http://www.fmwa.org

Georgia Movers Association, Inc.
113 Arkwright Landing
Macon, Georgia 31210
Phone: (478) 757-1325
http://www.georgiamovers.org

Illinois Movers & Warehousemen's Association
40 Adloff Lane, Suite 2
Springfield, IL 62703-4441
Phone: (217) 585-2470
http://www.imawa.com

Iowa Movers & Warehousemen's Association
717 East Court
Des Moines, IA 50392
Phone: (515) 244-5193
http://www.iowamotortruck.com

Kansas Motor Carriers Association
PO Box 1673
Topeka, KS 66601-1673
Phone: (785) 267-1641
http://www.kmca.org

Kentucky Household Goods Carriers Association
P.O. Box 22204
Louisville, KY 40252-0204
Phone: (502) 429-4957

Long Island Moving & Storage Association
P.O. Box 272, Southold, New York 11971
Phone: (631) 980-3882
http://www.limsa.com

Maryland Motor Truck Association, Inc.
3000 Washington Boulevard
Baltimore, MD 21230
Phone: (410) 644-4600
http://www.mmtanet.com

Massachusetts Movers Association
1 Robert Toner Blvd
North Attleboro, MA 02763
Phone: (508) 699-0023
http://www.massmovers.org

Michigan Movers & Warehousemen's Association
3225 W. St. Joseph
Lansing, MI 48917
Phone: (517) 327-9207
http://www.mimovers.org.

Minnesota Transport Services Association, Inc.
840 Hampden Ave., Suite 207
St. Paul, MN 55114
Phone: (651) 646-4075
http://www.mtsa.org

New Jersey Warehousemen & Movers Association & Tariff Bureau
94 East Water Street
Toms River, NJ 08753
Phone: (732) 341-3934
http://www.njwma.org

New Mexico Movers & Warehousemen's Association
P.O. Box 1153
Clovis, NM 88102-1153
Phone: (505) 763-3497
http://www.nmmwa.com

New York State Movers & Warehousemen's Association
45 South First Street
Brooklyn, New York, 11211
Phone: (800) 956 6966
http://www.newyorkmovers.com

North American Movers Association
6115 Stoney Creek Dr.
Ft. Wayne, IN 46818
Phone: (260) 483-1012
http://www.namovers.com

North Carolina Movers Association
P O Box 61210
Raleigh, NC 27661-1210
Phone: (800) 325-2114
http://www.ncmovers.org

Ohio Association of Movers, Inc.
5300 E. Main Street, Suite #104
Columbus, Ohio 43213
Phone: (614) 866-4349
http://www.ohiomovers.org

Oregon Moving & Storage Association
16303 NE Cameron Blvd.
Portland, Oregon 97230
Phone: (503) 236-1183
http://www.ormsa.com

Pennsylvania Moving & Storage Associates
c/o JWM Associates LLC
P.O. Box 526
Marlboro, NJ 07746
Phone: (732) 890-8563
http://www.pennmovers.org

Southwest Movers Association
700 East 11th Street
Austin, Texas 78701
Phone: (512) 476-0107
http://www.southwestmovers.org

Virginia Movers & Warehousemen's Association
1707 Summit Avenue, Suite 110
Richmond, Virginia 23230
Phone: (804) 358-1448
http://www.vmwa.org

Washington Movers Conference
930 South 336th St., Ste. B
Federal Way, WA 98003
Phone: (253) 838-1650
http://www.wmcmovers.com

Wisconsin Movers Association
562 Grand Canyon Dr
Madison, WI 53719
Phone: (608) 833-8200
http://www.wismovers.org

49 CFR § 370 et al

TITLE 49--TRANSPORTATION

CHAPTER III--FEDERAL MOTOR CARRIER SAFETY ADMINISTRATION, DEPARTMENT OF TRANSPORTATION

PART 370_PRINCIPLES AND PRACTICES FOR THE INVESTIGATION AND VOLUNTARY DISPOSITION OF LOSS AND DAMAGE CLAIMS AND PROCESSING SALVAGE—

Sec. 370.1 Applicability of regulations.

The regulations set forth in this part shall govern the processing of claims for loss, damage, injury, or delay to property transported or accepted for transportation, in interstate or foreign commerce, by each motor carrier, water carrier, and freight forwarder (hereinafter called carrier), subject to 49 U.S.C. subtitle IV, part B.

Sec. 370.3 Filing of claims.

(a) *Compliance with regulations.* A claim for loss or damage to baggage or for loss, damage, injury, or delay to cargo, shall not be voluntarily paid by a carrier unless filed, as provided in paragraph (b) of this section, with the receiving or delivering carrier, or carrier issuing the bill of lading, receipt, ticket, or baggage check, or carrier on whose line the alleged loss, damage, injury, or delay occurred, within the specified time limits applicable thereto and as otherwise may be required by law, the terms of the bill of lading or other contract of carriage, and all tariff provisions applicable thereto.

(b) *Minimum filing requirements.* A written or electronic communication (when agreed to by the carrier and shipper or receiver involved) from a claimant, filed with a proper carrier within the time limits specified in the bill of lading or contract of carriage or transportation and:

(1) Containing facts sufficient to identify the baggage or shipment (or shipments) of property,

(2) Asserting liability for alleged loss, damage, injury, or delay, and

(3) Making claim for the payment of a specified or determinable amount of money, shall be considered as sufficient compliance with the provisions for filing claims embraced in the bill of lading or other contract of carriage; *Provided, however,* That where claims are electronically handled, procedures are established to ensure reasonable carrier access to supporting documents.

(c) *Documents not constituting claims.* Bad order reports, appraisal reports of damage, notations of shortage or damage, or both, on freight bills, delivery receipts, or other documents, or inspection reports issued by carriers or their inspection agencies, whether the extent of loss or damage is indicated in dollars and cents or otherwise, shall, standing alone, not be considered by carriers as sufficient to comply with the minimum claim filing requirements specified in paragraph (b) of this section.

(d) *Claims filed for uncertain amounts.* Whenever a claim is presented against a proper carrier for an uncertain amount, such as "$100 more or less," the carrier against whom such claim is filed shall determine the condition of the baggage or shipment involved at the time of delivery by it, if it was delivered, and shall ascertain as nearly as possible the extent, if any, of the loss or damage for which it may be responsible. It shall not, however, voluntarily pay a claim under such circumstances unless and until a formal claim in writing for a specified or determinable amount of money shall have been filed in accordance with the provisions of paragraph (b) of this section.

(e) *Other claims.* If investigation of a claim develops that one or more other carriers has been presented with a similar claim on the same shipment, the carrier investigating such claim shall communicate with each such other carrier and, prior to any agreement entered into between or among them as to the proper disposition of such claim or claims, shall notify all claimants of the receipt of conflicting or overlapping claims and shall require further substantiation, on the part of each claimant of his/her title to the property involved or his/her right with respect to such claim.

Sec. 370.5 Acknowledgment of claims.

(a) Each carrier shall, upon receipt in writing or by electronic transmission of a proper claim in the manner and form described in the regulations in the past, acknowledge the receipt of such claim in writing or electronically to the claimant within 30 days after the date of its receipt by the carrier unless the carrier shall have paid or declined such claim in writing or electronically within 30 days of the receipt thereof. The carrier shall indicate in its acknowledgment to the claimant what, if any, additional documentary evidence or other pertinent information may be required by it further to process the claim as its preliminary examination of the claim, as filed, may have revealed.

(b) The carrier shall at the time each claim is received create a separate file and assign thereto a successive claim file number and note that number on all documents filed in support of the claim and all records and correspondence with respect to the claim, including the acknowledgment of receipt. At the time such claim is received the carrier shall cause the date of receipt to be recorded on the face of the claim document, and the date of receipt shall also appear in the carrier's acknowledgment of receipt to the claimant. The carrier shall also cause the claim file number to be noted on the shipping order, if in its possession, and the delivery receipt, if any, covering such shipment, unless the carrier has established an orderly and consistent internal procedure for assuring:

(1) That all information contained in shipping orders, delivery receipts, tally sheets, and all other pertinent records made with respect to the transportation of the shipment on which claim is made, is available for examination upon receipt of a claim;

(2) That all such records and documents (or true and complete reproductions thereof) are in fact examined in the course of the investigation of the claim (and an appropriate record is made that such examination has in fact taken place); and

(3) That such procedures prevent the duplicate or otherwise unlawful payment of claims.

Sec. 370.7 Investigation of claims.

(a) *Prompt investigation required.* Each claim filed against a carrier in the manner prescribed in this part shall be promptly and thoroughly investigated if investigation has not already been made prior to receipt of the claim.

(b) *Supporting documents.* When a necessary part of an investigation, each claim shall be supported by the original bill of lading, evidence of the freight charges, if any, and either the original invoice, a photographic copy of the original invoice, or an exact copy thereof or any extract made therefrom, certified by the claimant to be true and correct with respect to the property and value involved in the claim; or certification of prices or values, with trade or other discounts, allowance, or deductions, of any nature whatsoever and the terms thereof, or depreciation reflected thereon; *Provided, however,* That where property involved in a claim has not been invoiced to the consignee shown on the bill of lading or where an invoice does not show price or value, or where the property involved has been sold, or where the property has been transferred at bookkeeping values only, the carrier shall, before voluntarily paying a claim, require the claimant to establish the destination value in the quantity, shipped, transported, or involved; *Provided, further,* That when supporting documents are determined to be a necessary part of an investigation, the supporting documents are retained by the carriers for possible FMCSA inspection.

(c) *Verification of loss.* When an asserted claim for loss of an entire package or an entire shipment cannot be otherwise authenticated upon investigation, the carrier shall obtain from the consignee of the shipment involved a certified statement in writing that the property for which the claim is filed has not been received from any other source.

Sec. 370.9 Disposition of claims.

(a) Each carrier subject to 49 U.S.C. subtitle IV, part B which receives a written or electronically transmitted claim for loss or damage to baggage or for loss, damage, injury, or delay to property transported shall pay, decline, or make a firm compromise settlement offer in writing or electronically to the claimant within 120 days after receipt of the claim by the carrier; *Provided, however,* That, if the claim cannot be processed and disposed of within 120 days after the receipt thereof, the carrier shall at that time and at the expiration of each succeeding 60-day period while the claim remains pending, advise the claimant in writing or electronically of the status of the claim and the reason for the delay in making final disposition thereof and it shall retain a copy of such advice to the claimant in its claim file thereon.

(b) When settling a claim for loss or damage, a common carrier by motor vehicle of household goods as defined in §375.103 of this chapter shall use the replacement costs of the lost or damaged item as a base to apply a depreciation factor to arrive at the current actual value of the lost or damaged item: *Provided,* That where an item cannot be replaced or no suitable replacement is obtainable, the proper measure of damages shall be the original costs, augmented by a factor derived from a consumer price index, and adjusted downward by a factor depreciation over average useful life.

Sec. 370.11 Processing of salvage.

(a) Whenever baggage or material, goods, or other property transported by a carrier subject to the provisions in this part is damaged or alleged to be damaged and is, as a consequence thereof, not delivered or is rejected or refused upon tender thereof to the owner, consignee, or person entitled to receive such property, the carrier, after giving due notice, whenever practicable to do so, to the owner and other parties that may have an interest therein, and unless advised to the contrary after giving such notice, shall undertake to sell or dispose of such property directly or by the employment of a competent salvage agent. The carrier shall only dispose of the property in a manner that will fairly and equally protect the best interests of all persons having an interest therein. The carrier shall make an itemized record sufficient to identify the property involved so as to be able to correlate it to the shipment or transportation involved, and claim, if any, filed thereon. The carrier also shall assign to each lot of such property a successive lot number and note that lot number on its record of shipment and claim, if any claim is filed thereon.

(b) Whenever disposition of salvage material or goods shall be made directly to an agent or employee of a carrier or through a salvage agent or company in which the carrier or one or more of its directors, officers, or managers has any interest, financial or otherwise, that carrier's salvage records shall fully reflect the particulars of each such transaction or relationship, or both, as the case may be.

(c) Upon receipt of a claim on a shipment on which salvage has been processed in the manner prescribed in this section, the carrier shall record in its claim file thereon the lot number assigned, the amount of money recovered, if any, from the disposition of such property, and the date of transmittal of such money to the person or persons lawfully entitled to receive the same.

49 CFR § 371 et al

TITLE 49--TRANSPORTATION

CHAPTER III--FEDERAL MOTOR CARRIER SAFETY ADMINISTRATION,

DEPARTMENT OF TRANSPORTATION

PART 371 BROKERS OF PROPERTY

Subpart A
General Requirements

Sec. 371.1 Applicability.

This part applies, to the extent provided therein, to all brokers of transportation by motor vehicle as defined in §371.2.

Sec. 371.2 Definitions.

(a) *Broker* means a person who, for compensation, arranges, or offers to arrange, the transportation of property by an authorized motor carrier. Motor carriers, or persons who are employees or bona fide agents of carriers, are not brokers within the meaning of this section when they arrange or offer to arrange the transportation of shipments which they are authorized to transport and which they have accepted and legally bound themselves to transport.

(b) *Bona fide agents* are persons who are part of the normal organization of a motor carrier and perform duties under the carrier's directions pursuant to a preexisting agreement which provides for a continuing relationship, precluding the exercise of discretion on the part of the agent in allocating traffic between the carrier and others.

(c) *Brokerage* or *brokerage service* is the arranging of transportation or the physical movement of a motor vehicle or of property. It can be performed on behalf of a motor carrier, consignor, or consignee.

(d) *Non-brokerage service* is all other service performed by a broker on behalf of a motor carrier, consignor, or consignee.

Sec. 371.3 Records to be kept by brokers.

(a) A broker shall keep a record of each transaction. For purposes of this section, brokers may keep master lists of consignors and the address and registration number of the carrier, rather than repeating this information for each transaction. The record shall show:

(1) The name and address of the consignor;

(2) The name, address, and registration number of the originating motor carrier;

(3) The bill of lading or freight bill number;

(4) The amount of compensation received by the broker for the brokerage service performed and the name of the payer;

(5) A description of any non-brokerage service performed in connection with each shipment or other activity, the amount of compensation received for the service, and the name of the payer; and

(6) The amount of any freight charges collected by the broker and the date of payment to the carrier.

(b) Brokers shall keep the records required by this section for a period of three years.

(c) Each party to a brokered transaction has the right to review the record of the transaction required to be kept by these rules.

Sec. 371.7 Misrepresentation.

(a) A broker shall not perform or offer to perform any brokerage service (including advertising), in any name other than that in which its registration is issued.

(b) A broker shall not, directly or indirectly, represent its operations to be that of a carrier. Any advertising shall show the broker status of the operation.

Sec. 371.9 Rebating and compensation.

(a) A broker shall not charge or receive compensation from a motor carrier for brokerage service where:

(1) The broker owns or has a material beneficial interest in the shipment or

(2) The broker is able to exercise control over the shipment because the broker owns the shipper, the shipper owns the broker, or there is common ownership of the two.

(b) A broker shall not give or offer to give anything of value to any shipper, consignor or consignee (or their officers or employees) except inexpensive advertising items given for promotional purposes.

Sec. 371.10 Duties and obligations of brokers.

Where the broker acts on behalf of a person bound by law or the FMCSA regulation as to the transmittal of bills or payments, the broker must also abide by the law or regulations which apply to that person.

Sec. 371.13 Accounting.

Each broker who engages in any other business shall maintain accounts so that the revenues and expenses relating to the brokerage portion of its business are segregated from its other activities. Expenses that are common shall be allocated on an equitable basis; however, the broker must be prepared to explain the basis for the allocation.

Subpart B
Special Rules for Household Goods Brokers

§371.101 If I operate as a household goods broker in interstate or foreign commerce, must I comply with subpart B of this part?

Yes, you must comply with all regulations in this subpart when you operate as a household goods broker offering services to individual shippers in interstate or foreign commerce. The regulations in this subpart do not apply to a household goods broker when providing services to commercial or government shippers in interstate or foreign commerce.

§371.103 What are the definitions of terms used in this subpart?

FMCSA means the Federal Motor Carrier Safety Administration within the U.S. Department of Transportation.

Household goods has the same meaning as the term is defined in §375.103 of this subchapter.

Household goods broker means a person, other than a motor carrier or an employee or bona fide agent of a motor carrier, that as a principal or agent sells, offers for sale, negotiates for, or holds itself out by solicitation, advertisement, or otherwise as selling, providing, or arranging for, transportation of household goods by motor carrier for compensation.

Individual shipper has the same meaning as the term is defined in §375.103 of this subchapter.

§371.105 Must I use a motor carrier that has a valid U.S. DOT number and valid operating authority issued by FMCSA to transport household goods in interstate or foreign commerce?

You may only act as a household goods broker for a motor carrier that has a valid, active U.S. DOT number and valid operating authority issued by FMCSA to transport household goods in interstate or foreign commerce.

§371.107 What information must I display in my advertisements and Internet Web homepage?

(a) You must prominently display in your advertisements and Internet Web homepage(s) the physical location(s) (street or highway address, city, and State) where you conduct business.

(b) You must prominently display your U.S. DOT registration number(s) and MC license number issued by the FMCSA in your advertisements and Internet Web homepage(s).

(c) You must prominently display in your advertisements and Internet Web site(s) your status as a household goods broker and the statement that you will not transport an individual shipper's household goods, but that you will arrange for the transportation of the household goods by an FMCSA-authorized household goods motor carrier, whose charges will be determined by its published tariff.

(d) If you provide estimates on any carrier's behalf pursuant to §371.113(b), you must prominently display in your Internet Web site(s) that the estimate must be based on the carrier's tariff and that the carrier is required to make its tariff available for public inspection upon a reasonable request.

(e) You may only include in your advertisements or Internet Web site(s) the names or logos of FMCSA-authorized household goods motor carriers with whom you have a written agreement as specified in §371.115 of this part.

§371.109 Must I inform individual shippers which motor carriers I use?

(a) You must provide to each potential individual shipper who contacts you a list of all authorized household goods motor carriers you use, including their U.S. DOT registration number(s) and MC license numbers. You may provide the list electronically or on paper.

(b) You must provide to each potential individual shipper who contacts you a statement indicating that you are not a motor carrier authorized by the Federal Government to transport the individual shipper's household goods, and you are only arranging for an authorized household goods motor carrier to perform the transportation services and, if applicable, additional services. You may provide the statement electronically or on paper.

§371.111 Must I provide individual shippers with Federal consumer protection information?

(a) You must provide potential individual shippers with Federal consumer protection information by one of the following three methods:

(1) Provide a hyperlink on your Internet Web site to the FMCSA Web site containing the information in FMCSA's publications "Ready to Move?—Tips for a Successful Interstate Move" and "Your Rights and Responsibilities When You Move."

(2) Distribute to each shipper and potential shipper at the time you provide an estimate, copies of FMCSA's publications "Ready to Move?—Tips for a Successful Interstate Move" and "Your Rights and Responsibilities When You Move."

(3) Distribute to each shipper and potential shipper at the time you provide an estimate, copies of "Ready to Move?—Tips for a Successful Interstate Move" and "Your Rights and Responsibilities When You Move" as modified and produced by the authorized, lawful motor carrier to which you intend to provide the shipment under your written agreement required by §371.115.

(b) If an individual shipper elects to waive physical receipt of the Federal consumer protection information by one of the methods described in paragraphs (a)(2) and (a)(3) of this section, and elects to access the same information via the hyperlink on the Internet as provided in paragraph (a)(1) of this section, you must include a clear and concise statement on the written estimate described in §371.113 that the individual shipper expressly agreed to access the Federal consumer protection information on the Internet.

(c) You must obtain a signed, dated, electronic or paper receipt showing the individual shipper has received both booklets that includes, if applicable, verification of the shipper's agreement to access the Federal consumer protection information on the Internet.

(d) You must maintain the signed receipt required by paragraph (c) of this section for three years from the date the individual shipper signs the receipt.

§371.113 May I provide individual shippers with a written estimate?

(a) You may provide each individual shipper with an estimate of transportation and accessorial charges. If you provide an estimate, it must be in writing and must be based on a physical survey of the household goods conducted by the authorized motor carrier on whose behalf the estimate is provided if the goods are located within a 50-mile radius of the motor carrier's or its agent's location, whichever is closer. The estimate must be prepared in accordance with a signed, written agreement, as specified in §371.115 of this subpart.

(b) You must base your estimate upon the published tariffs of the authorized motor carrier who will transport the shipper's household goods.

(c)(1) A shipper may elect to waive the physical survey required in paragraph (a) of this section by written agreement signed by the shipper before the shipment is loaded.

(2) The household goods broker must explain the physical survey waiver agreement to the individual shipper in plain English. The physical survey waiver agreement must be printed on the written estimate and must be printed at no less than 7-point font size and with the font typeface Universe.

(3) A copy of the waiver agreement must be retained as an addendum to the bill of lading and is subject to the same record inspection and preservation requirements as are applicable to bills of lading.

(d) You must keep the records required by this section for three years following the date you provide the written estimate for an individual shipper who accepts the estimate and has you procure the transportation.

§371.115 Must I maintain agreements with motor carriers before providing written estimates on behalf of these carriers?

(a) In order to provide estimates of charges for the transportation of household goods, you must do so in accordance with the written agreement required by

§375.409 of this subchapter. Your written agreement with the motor carrier(s) must include the following items:

(1) Your broker name as shown on your FMCSA registration, your physical address, and your U.S. DOT registration number and MC license number;

(2) The authorized motor carrier's name as shown on its FMCSA registration, its physical address, and its U.S. DOT registration number and MC license number;

(3) A concise, easy to understand statement that your written estimate to the individual shipper:

(i) Will be exclusively on behalf of the authorized household goods motor carrier;

(ii) Will be based on the authorized household goods motor carrier's published tariff; and

(iii) Will serve as the authorized household goods motor carrier's estimate for purposes of complying with the requirements of part 375 of this chapter, including the requirement that the authorized household goods motor carrier relinquishes possession of the shipment upon payment of no more than 110 percent of a non-binding estimate at the time of delivery;

(4) Your owner's, corporate officer's, or corporate director's signature lawfully representing your household goods broker operation and the date;

(5) The signature of the authorized household goods motor carrier's owner, corporate officer, or corporate director lawfully representing the household goods motor carrier's operation and the date; and

(b) The signed written agreement required by this section is public information and you must produce it for review upon reasonable request by a member of the public.

(c) You must keep copies of the agreements required by this section for as long as you provide estimates on behalf of the authorized household goods motor carrier and for three years thereafter.

§371.117 *Must I provide individual shippers with my policies concerning cancellation, deposits, and refunds?*

(a) You must disclose prominently on your Internet Web site and in your agreements with prospective shippers your cancellation policy, deposit policy, and policy for refunding deposited funds in the event the shipper cancels an order for service before the date an authorized household goods motor carrier has been scheduled to pick up the shipper's property.

(b) You must maintain records showing each individual shipper's request to cancel a shipment and the disposition of each request for a period of three years after the date of a shipper's cancellation request. If you refunded a deposit, your records must include:

(1) Proof that the individual shipper cashed or deposited the check or money order, if the financial institution provides documentary evidence; or

(2) Proof that you delivered the refund check or money order to the individual shipper.

§371.121 *What penalties may FMCSA impose for violations of this part?*

The penalty provisions of 49 U.S.C. chapter 149, *Civil and Criminal Penalties* apply to this subpart. These penalties do not overlap. Notwithstanding these civil penalties, nothing in this section deprives an individual shipper of any remedy or right of action under existing law.

49 CFR § 375 et al

TITLE 49--TRANSPORTATION

CHAPTER III--FEDERAL MOTOR CARRIER SAFETY ADMINISTRATION,

DEPARTMENT OF TRANSPORTATION

PART 375 TRANSPORTATION OF HOUSEHOLD GOODS IN INTERSTATE COMMERCE; CONSUMER PROTECTION REGULATIONS--Table of Contents

Subpart A
General Requirements

§375.101 Who must follow the regulations in this part?

You, a household goods motor carrier engaged in the interstate transportation of household goods, must follow the regulations in this part when offering your services to individual shippers. You are subject to this part only when you transport household goods for individual shippers by motor vehicle in interstate commerce. Interstate commerce is defined in §390.5 of this subchapter.

§375.103 What are the definitions of terms used in this part?

Terms used in this part are defined as follows. You may find other terms used in these regulations defined in 49 U.S.C. 13102. The definitions contained in this statute control. If terms are used in this part and the terms are neither defined here nor in 49 U.S.C. 13102, the terms will have the ordinary practical meaning of such terms.

Advertisement means any communication to the public in connection with an offer or sale of any interstate household goods transportation service. This includes written or electronic database listings of your name, address, and telephone number in an on-line database or displayed on an Internet web site. This excludes listings of your name, address, and telephone number in a telephone directory or similar publication. However, Yellow Pages advertising is included in the definition.

Cashier's check means a check that has all four of the following characteristics:

(1) Drawn on a bank as defined in 12 CFR 229.2.

(2) Signed by an officer or employee of the bank on behalf of the bank as drawer.

(3) A direct obligation of the bank.

(4) Provided to a customer of the bank or acquired from the bank for remittance purposes.

Certified scale means any scale inspected and certified by an authorized scale inspection and licensing authority, and designed for weighing motor vehicles, including trailers or semi-trailers not attached to a tractor, or designed as a platform or warehouse type scale.

Commercial shipper means any person who is named as the consignor or consignee in a bill of lading contract who is not the owner of the goods being transported but who assumes the responsibility for payment of the transportation and other tariff charges for the account of the beneficial owner of the goods. The beneficial owner of the goods is normally an employee of the consignor and/or consignee. A freight forwarder tendering a shipment to a carrier in furtherance of freight forwarder operations is also a commercial shipper. The Federal government is a government bill of lading shipper, not a commercial shipper.

Force majeure means a defense protecting the parties in the event that a part of the contract cannot be performed due to causes which are outside the control of the parties and could not be avoided by exercise of due care.

Government bill of lading shipper means any person whose property is transported under the terms and conditions of a government bill of lading issued by any department or agency of the Federal government to the carrier responsible for the transportation of the shipment.

Household goods, as used in connection with transportation, means the personal effects or property used, or to be used, in a dwelling, when part of the equipment or supplies of the dwelling. Transportation of the household goods must be arranged and paid for by the individual shipper or by another individual on behalf of the shipper. Household goods includes property moving from a factory or store if purchased with the intent to use in a dwelling and transported at the request of the householder, who also pays the transportation charges.

***Household goods motor carrier* means—**

(1) In general, a motor carrier that, in the ordinary course of its business of providing transportation of household goods, offers some or all of the following additional services:

(i) Binding and nonbinding estimates;

(ii) Inventorying;

(iii) Protective packing and unpacking of individual items at personal residences;

(iv) Loading and unloading at personal residences.

(2) The term includes any person considered to be a household goods motor carrier under regulations, determinations, and decisions of the Federal Motor Carrier Safety Administration in effect on the date of enactment of the Household Goods Mover Oversight Enforcement and Reform Act of 2005 (August 10, 2005).

(3) The term does not include any motor carrier providing transportation of household goods in containers or trailers that are entirely loaded and unloaded by an individual other than an employee or agent of the motor carrier.

(4) The term does not include any motor carrier that acts as a service for the delivery of furniture, appliances, or other furnishings between a factory or a store and an individual's household.

Individual shipper means any person who—

(1) Is the shipper, consignor, or consignee of a household goods shipment;

(2) Is identified as the shipper, consignor, or consignee on the face of the bill of lading;

(3) Owns the goods being transported; and

(4) Pays his or her own tariff transportation charges

May means an option. You may do something, but it is not a requirement.

Must means a legal obligation. You must do something.

Order for service means a document authorizing you to transport an individual shipper's household goods.

Reasonable dispatch means the performance of transportation on the dates, or during the period, agreed upon by you and the individual shipper and shown on the Order For Service/Bill of Lading. For example, if you deliberately withhold any shipment from delivery after an individual shipper offers to pay the binding estimate or 110 percent of a non-binding estimate, you have not transported the goods with reasonable dispatch. The term "reasonable dispatch" excludes transportation provided under your tariff provisions requiring guaranteed service dates. You will have the defenses of force majeure, *i.e.*, superior or irresistible force, as construed by the courts.

Should means a recommendation. We recommend you do something, but it is not a requirement.

Surface Transportation Board means an agency within the Department of Transportation. The Surface Transportation Board regulates household goods carrier tariffs among other responsibilities.

Tariff means an issuance (in whole or in part) containing rates, rules, regulations, classifications or other provisions related to a motor carrier's transportation services. The Surface Transportation Board requires a tariff contain specific items under §1312.3(a) of this title. These specific items include an accurate description of the services offered to the public and the specific applicable rates (or the basis for calculating the specific applicable rates) and service terms. A tariff must be arranged in a way that allows for the determination of the exact rate(s) and service terms applicable to any given shipment.

We, us, and our means the Federal Motor Carrier Safety Administration (FMCSA).

You and *your* means a household goods motor carrier engaged in the interstate transportation of household goods and its household goods agents.

§375.105 What are the information collection requirements of this part?

(a) The information collection requirements of this part have been reviewed by the Office of Management and Budget pursuant to the Paperwork Reduction Act of 1995 (44 U.S.C. 3501 *et seq.*) and have been assigned OMB control number 2126-0025.

(b) The information collection requirements are found in the following sections: §§375.205, 375.207, 375.209,

375.211, 375.213, 375.215, 375.217, 375.303, 375.401, 375.403, 375.405, 375.409, 375.501, 375.503, 375.505, 375.507, 375.515, 375.519, 375.521, 375.605, 375.607, 375.609, 375.803, 375.805, and 375.807.

Subpart B
Before Offering Services to My Customers

§375.201 What is my normal liability for loss and damage when I accept goods from an individual shipper?

(a) In general, you are legally liable for loss or damage if it happens during performance of any transportation of household goods and all related services identified on your lawful bill of lading.

(b) Full Value Protection Obligation—In general, your liability is for the household goods that are lost, damaged, destroyed, or otherwise not delivered to the final destination in an amount equal to the replacement value of the household goods. The maximum amount is the declared value of the shipment. The declared value is subject to rules issued by the Surface Transportation Board (STB) and applicable tariffs.

(c) If the shipper waives, in writing, your liability for the full value of the household goods, then you are liable for loss of, or damage to, any household goods to the extent provided in the STB released rates order. Contact the STB for a current copy of the Released Rates of Motor Carrier Shipments of Household Goods. The rate may be increased annually by the motor carrier based on the U.S. Department of Commerce's Cost of Living Adjustment.

(d) As required by §375.303(g), you may have additional liability if you sell liability insurance and fail to issue a copy of the insurance policy or other appropriate evidence of insurance.

(e) You must, in a clear and concise manner, disclose to the individual shipper the limits of your liability.

§375.203 What actions of an individual shipper may limit or reduce my normal liability?

(a) If an individual shipper includes perishable, dangerous, or hazardous articles in the shipment without your knowledge, you need not assume liability for those articles or for the loss or damage caused by their inclusion in the shipment. If the shipper requests that you accept such articles for transportation, you may elect to limit your liability for any loss or damage by appropriately published tariff provisions.

(b) If an individual shipper agrees to ship household goods released at a value greater than 60 cents per pound ($1.32 per kilogram) per article, your liability for loss and damage may be limited to $100 per pound ($220 per kilogram) per article if the individual shipper fails to notify you in writing of articles valued at more than $100 per pound ($220 per kilogram).

(c) If an individual shipper notifies you in writing that an article valued at greater than $100 per pound ($220 per kilogram) will be included in the shipment, the shipper will be entitled to full recovery up to the declared value of the article or articles, not to exceed the declared value of the entire shipment.

General Responsibilities

§375.205 May I have agents?

(a) You may have agents provided you comply with paragraphs (b) and (c) of this section. A household goods agent is defined as either one of the following two types of agents:

(1) A *prime agent* provides a transportation service for you or on your behalf, including the selling of, or arranging for, a transportation service. You permit or require the agent to provide services under the terms of an agreement or arrangement with you. A prime agent does not provide services on an emergency or temporary basis. A prime agent does not include a household goods broker or freight forwarder.

(2) An *emergency or temporary agent* provides origin or destination services on your behalf,

excluding the selling of, or arranging for, a transportation service. You permit or require the agent to provide such services under the terms of an agreement or arrangement with you. The agent performs such services only on an emergency or temporary basis.

(b) If you have agents, you must have written agreements between you and your prime agents. You and your retained prime agent must sign the agreements.

(c) Copies of all your prime agent agreements must be in your files for a period of at least 24 months following the date of termination of each agreement.

§375.207 What items must be in my advertisements?

(a) You and your agents must publish and use only truthful, straightforward, and honest advertisements.

(b) You must include, and you must require each of your agents to include, in all advertisements for all services (including any accessorial services incidental to or part of interstate household goods transportation), the following two elements:

(1) Your name or trade name, as it appears on our document assigning you a U.S. DOT number, or the name or trade name of the motor carrier under whose operating authority the advertised service will originate.

(2) Your U.S. DOT number, assigned by us authorizing you to operate as a for-hire motor carrier transporting household goods.

(c) Your FMCSA-assigned U.S. DOT number must be displayed only in the following form in every advertisement: U.S. DOT No. (*assigned number*).

§375.209 How must I handle complaints and inquiries?

(a) You must establish and maintain a procedure for responding to complaints and inquiries from your individual shippers.

(b) Your procedure must include all three of the following items:

(1) A communications system allowing individual shippers to communicate with your principal place of business by telephone.

(2) A telephone number.

(3) A written or electronic record system for recording all inquiries and complaints received from an individual shipper by any means of communication.

(c) You must produce a clear and concise written description of your procedure for distribution to individual shippers.

§375.211 Must I have an arbitration program?

(a) You must have an arbitration program for individual shippers to resolve disputes about property loss and damage and disputes about whether carrier charges in addition to those collected at delivery must be paid. You must establish and maintain an arbitration program with the following 11 minimum elements:

(1) You must design your arbitration program to prevent you from having any special advantage in any case where the claimant resides or does business at a place distant from your principal or other place of business.

(2) Before execution of the order for service, you must provide notice to the individual shipper of the availability of neutral arbitration, including all three of the following items:

(i) A summary of the arbitration procedure.

(ii) Any applicable costs.

(iii) A disclosure of the legal effects of election to use arbitration.

(3) Upon the individual shipper's request, you must provide information and forms you consider necessary for initiating an action to resolve a dispute under arbitration.

(4) You must require each person you authorize to arbitrate to be independent of the parties to the dispute and capable of resolving such disputes, and

you must ensure the arbitrator is authorized and able to obtain from you or the individual shipper any material or relevant information to carry out a fair and expeditious decision making process.

(5) You must not charge the individual shipper more than one-half of the total cost for instituting the arbitration proceeding against you. In the arbitrator's decision, the arbitrator may determine which party must pay the cost or a portion of the cost of the arbitration proceeding, including the cost of instituting the proceeding.

(6) You must refrain from requiring the individual shipper to agree to use arbitration before a dispute arises.

(7) Arbitration must be binding for claims of $10,000 or less, if the individual shipper requests arbitration.

(8) Arbitration must be binding for claims of more than $10,000, if the individual shipper requests arbitration and the carrier agrees to it.

(9) If all parties agree, the arbitrator may provide for an oral presentation of a dispute by a party or representative of a party.

(10) The arbitrator must render a decision within 60 days of receipt of written notification of the dispute, and a decision by an arbitrator may include any remedies appropriate under the circumstances.

(11) The arbitrator may extend the 60-day period for a reasonable period if you or the individual shipper fail to provide, in a timely manner, any information the arbitrator reasonably requires to resolve the dispute.

(b) You must produce and distribute a concise, easy-to-read, accurate summary of your arbitration program, including the items in this section.

§375.213 What information must I provide to a prospective individual shipper?

(a) When you provide the written estimate to a prospective individual shipper, you must also provide the individual shipper with a copy of Department of Transportation publication FMCSA-ESA-03-005 (or its successor publication) entitled "Ready to Move?—Tips for a Successful Interstate Move." You may provide the individual shipper with a paper copy or you may provide a hyperlink on your Internet Web site to the FMCSA Web site containing the information in FMCSA's publication "Ready to Move?—Tips for a Successful Interstate Move."

(b) Before you execute an order for service for a shipment of household goods, you must furnish to your prospective individual shipper all five of the following documents:

(1) The contents of appendix A of this part, entitled "Your Rights and Responsibilities When You Move" (Department of Transportation publication FMCSA-ESA-03-006, or its successor publication). You may provide the individual shipper with a paper copy or you may provide a hyperlink on your Internet Web site to the FMCSA Web site containing the information in FMCSA's publication "Your Rights and Responsibilities When You Move."

(2) A concise, easy-to-read, accurate estimate of your charges.

(3) A notice of the availability of the applicable sections of your tariff for the estimate of charges, including an explanation that individual shippers may examine these tariff sections or have copies sent to them upon request.

(4) A concise, easy-to-read, accurate summary of your arbitration program.

(5) A concise, easy-to-read, accurate summary of your customer complaint and inquiry handling procedures. Included in this description must be both of the following two items:

(i) The main telephone number the individual shipper may use to communicate with you.

(ii) A clear and concise statement concerning who must pay for telephone calls.

(c) To comply with paragraph (b)(1) of this section, you must ensure that the text and general order of the document you produce and distribute to prospective individual shippers are consistent with the text and general order of appendix A to this part. The following three items also apply:

(1) If we, the Federal Motor Carrier Safety Administration, choose to modify the text or general order of appendix A, we will provide the public appropriate notice in the FEDERAL REGISTER and an opportunity for comment as required by part 389 of this chapter before making you change anything.

(2) If you publish the document, you may choose the dimensions of the publication as long as the type font size is 10 points or larger and the size of the booklet is at least as large as 36 square inches (232 square centimeters).

(3) If you publish the document, you may choose the color and design of the front and back covers of the publication. The following words must appear prominently on the front cover in 12-point or larger bold or full-faced type: "Your Rights and Responsibilities When You Move. Furnished by Your Mover, as Required by Federal Law." You may substitute your name or trade name in place of "Your Mover" if you wish (for example, *Furnished by XYZ Van Lines, as Required by Federal Law*).

(d) Paragraphs (c)(2) and (c)(3) of this section do not apply to exact copies of appendix A published in the FEDERAL REGISTER, the Code of Federal Regulations, or on FMCSA's Web site.

(e) If an individual shipper elects to waive physical receipt of the Federal consumer protection information by one of the methods described in paragraphs (a) and (b)(1) of this section, and elects to access the same information via the hyperlink on the Internet as provided in paragraphs (a) and (b)(1) of this section:

(1) You must include a clear and concise statement on the written estimate described in §375.401 that the individual shipper expressly agreed to access the Federal consumer protection information on the Internet.

(2) You must obtain a signed, dated, electronic or paper receipt showing the individual shipper has received both booklets that includes, if applicable, verification of the shipper's agreement to access the Federal consumer protection information on the Internet.

(3) You must maintain the signed receipt required by paragraph (e)(2) of this section for one year

from the date the individual shipper signs the receipt. You are not required to maintain the signed receipt when you do not actually transport household goods or perform related services for the individual shipper who signed the receipt.

§375.215 How must I collect charges?

You must issue an honest, truthful freight or expense bill in accordance with subpart A of part 373 of this chapter. All rates and charges for the transportation and related services must be in accordance with your appropriately published tariff provisions in effect, including the method of payment.

§375.217 How must I collect charges upon delivery?

(a) You must specify the form of payment when you prepare the estimate. You and your agents must honor the form of payment at delivery, except when a shipper agrees to a change in writing.

(b) You must specify the same form of payment provided in paragraph (a) of this section when you prepare the order for service and the bill of lading.

(c) Charge or credit card payments:

(1) If you agree to accept payment by charge or credit card, you must arrange with the individual shipper for the delivery only at a time when you can obtain authorization for the shipper's credit card transaction.

(2) Paragraph (c)(1) of this section does not apply to you when you have equipped your motor vehicle(s) to process card transactions.

(d) You may maintain a tariff setting forth nondiscriminatory rules governing collect-on-delivery service and the collection of collect-on-delivery funds.

(e) If an individual shipper pays you at least 110 percent of the approximate costs of a non-binding estimate on a collect-on-delivery shipment, you must relinquish possession of the shipment at the time of delivery.

§375.219 May I extend credit to shippers?

You may extend credit to shippers, but, if you do, it must be in accordance with §375.807.

§375.221 May I use a charge or credit card plan for payments?

(a) You may provide in your tariff for the acceptance of charge or credit cards for the payment of freight charges. Accepting charge or credit card payments is different than extending credit to shippers in §§375.219 and 375.807. Once you provide an estimate you are bound by the provisions in your tariff regarding payment as of the estimate date, until completion of any transaction that results from that estimate, unless otherwise agreed with a shipper under §375.217(a).

(b) You may accept charge or credit cards whenever shipments are transported under agreements and tariffs requiring payment by cash, certified check, money order, or a cashier's check.

(c) If you allow an individual shipper to pay for a freight or expense bill by charge or credit card, you are deeming such payment to be the same as payment by cash, certified check, money order, or a cashier's check.

(d) The charge or credit card plans you participate in must be identified in your tariff rules as items permitting the acceptance of the charge or credit cards.

(e) If an individual shipper causes a charge or credit card issuer to reverse a charge transaction, you may consider the individual shipper's action tantamount to forcing you to provide an involuntary extension of your credit. In such instances, the rules in §375.807 apply.

Subpart C
Service Options Provided

§375.301 What service options may I provide?

(a) You may design your household goods service to provide individual shippers with a wide range of specialized service and pricing features. Many carriers provide at least the following five service options:

(1) Space reservation.

(2) Expedited service.

(3) Exclusive use of a vehicle.

(4) Guaranteed service on or between agreed dates.

(5) Liability insurance.

(b) If you sell liability insurance, you must follow the requirements in §375.303.

§375.303 If I sell liability insurance coverage, what must I do?

(a) You, your employee, or an agent may sell, offer to sell, or procure liability insurance coverage for loss or damage to shipments of any individual shipper only when the individual shipper releases the shipment for transportation at a value not exceeding 60 cents per pound ($1.32 per kilogram) per article.

(b) You may offer, sell, or procure any type of insurance policy on behalf of the individual shipper covering loss or damage in excess of the specified carrier liability.

(c) If you sell, offer to sell, or procure liability insurance coverage for loss or damage to shipments:

(1) You must issue to the individual shipper a policy or other appropriate evidence of the insurance that the individual shipper purchased.

(2) You must provide a copy of the policy or other appropriate evidence to the individual shipper at the time you sell or procure the insurance.

(3) You must issue policies written in plain English.

(4) You must clearly specify the nature and extent of coverage under the policy.

(5) Your failure to issue a policy, or other appropriate evidence of insurance purchased, to an individual shipper will subject you to full liability for any claims to recover loss or damage attributed to you.

(6) You must provide in your tariff for the provision of selling, offering to sell, or procuring liability insurance coverage. The tariff must also provide for the base transportation charge, including your assumption of full liability for the value of the shipment. This would be in the event you fail to issue a policy or other appropriate evidence of insurance to the individual shipper at the time of purchase.

Subpart D
Estimating Charges

§375.401 Must I estimate charges?

(a) You must conduct a physical survey of the household goods to be transported and provide the prospective individual shipper with a written estimate, based on the physical survey, of the charges for the transportation and all related services. There are *two exceptions* to the requirement to conduct a physical survey:

(1) If the household goods are located beyond a 50-mile radius of the location of the household goods motor carrier's agent preparing the estimate, the requirement to base the estimate on a physical survey does not apply.

(2) An individual shipper may elect to waive the physical survey. The waiver agreement is subject to the following requirements:

(i) It must be in writing;

(ii) It must be signed by the shipper before the shipment is loaded; and

(iii) The household goods motor carrier must retain a copy of the waiver agreement as an addendum to the bill of lading with the understanding that the waiver agreement will be subject to the same record retention requirements that apply to bills of lading, as provided in §375.505(d).

(b) Before you execute an order for service for a shipment of household goods for an individual shipper, you must provide a written estimate of the total charges and *indicate whether it is a binding or a non-binding estimate*, as follows:

(1) *A binding estimate* is an agreement made in advance with your individual shipper. It guarantees the total cost of the move based upon the quantities and services shown on your estimate, which shall be based on the physical survey of the household goods, if required. You may impose a charge for providing a written binding estimate. The binding estimate must indicate that you and the shipper are bound by the charges.

(2) *A non-binding estimate* is what you believe the total cost will be for the move, based upon both the estimated weight or volume of the shipment and the accessorial services requested and the physical survey of the household goods, if required. A non-binding estimate is not binding on you. You will base the final charges upon the actual weight of the individual shipper's shipment and the tariff provisions in effect. You may not impose a charge for providing a non-binding estimate.

(c) You must specify the form of payment you and your agent will honor at delivery. Payment forms may include, but are not limited to, cash, a certified check, a money order, a cashier s check, a specific charge card such as American ExpressTM, a specific credit card such as VisaTM, or your credit as allowed by §375.807.

(d) For non-binding estimates, you must provide your reasonably accurate estimate of the approximate costs the individual shipper should expect to pay for the transportation and services of such shipments. If you provide an inaccurately low estimate, you may be limiting the amount you will collect at the time of delivery as provided in §375.407.

(e) If you provide a shipper with an estimate based on volume that will later be converted to a weight-based rate, you must provide the shipper an explanation in writing of the formula used to calculate the conversion to weight. You must specify the final charges will be based on actual weight and services subject to the 110 percent rule at delivery.

(f) You must determine charges for any accessorial services such as elevators, long carries, etc., before preparing the order for service and the bill of lading for binding or non-binding estimates. If you fail to ask the shipper about such charges and fail to determine such charges before preparing the order for service and the bill of lading, you must deliver the goods and bill the shipper after 30 days for the additional charges.

(g) You must include as a part of your estimate the liability election notice provided in the Surface Transportation Board's released rates order. Contact the STB for a copy of the Released Rates of Motor Carrier Shipments of Household Goods.

(h) You and the individual shipper must sign the estimate of charges. You must provide a dated copy of the estimate of charges to the individual shipper at the time you sign the estimate.

(i) Before loading a household goods shipment, and upon mutual agreement of both you and the individual shipper, you may amend an estimate of charges. You may not amend the estimate after loading the shipment.

§375.403 How must I provide a binding estimate?

(a) You may provide a guaranteed binding estimate of the total shipment charges to the individual shipper, so long as it is provided for in your tariff. The individual shipper must pay the amount for the services included in your estimate. You must comply with the following 11 requirements:

(1) You must base the binding estimate on the physical survey unless one of the exceptions provided in §375.401(a)(1) and (2) applies.

(2) You must provide the binding estimate in writing to the individual shipper or other person responsible for payment of the freight charges.

(3) You must retain a copy of each binding estimate as an attachment to be made an integral part of the bill of lading contract.

(4) You must clearly indicate upon each binding estimate's face that the estimate is binding upon you and the individual shipper. Each binding estimate must also clearly indicate on its face that the charges shown apply only to those services specifically identified in the estimate.

(5) You must clearly describe binding-estimate shipments and all services you are providing.

(6) If it appears an individual shipper has tendered additional household goods or requires additional services not identified in the binding estimate, you are not required to honor the estimate. If an agreement cannot be reached as to the price or service requirements for the additional goods or services, you are not required to service the shipment. However, if you do service the shipment, before loading the shipment you must do one of the following three things:

(i) Reaffirm your binding estimate.

(ii) Negotiate a revised written binding estimate accurately listing, in detail, the additional household goods or services.

(iii) Agree with the individual shipper, in writing, that both of you will consider the original binding estimate as a non-binding estimate subject to §375.405.

(7) Once you load a shipment, failure to execute a new binding estimate or a non-binding estimate signifies you have reaffirmed the original binding estimate. You may not collect more than the amount of the original binding estimate, except as provided in paragraphs (a)(8) and (9) of this section.

(8) If you believe additional services are necessary to properly service a shipment after the bill of lading has been issued, you must inform the individual shipper what the additional services are before performing those services. You must allow the shipper at least one hour to determine whether he or she wants the additional services performed. If the individual shipper agrees to pay for the additional services, you must execute a written attachment to be made an integral part of the bill of lading contract and have the individual shipper

sign the written attachment. This may be done through fax transmissions; e-mail; overnight courier; or certified mail, return receipt requested. You must bill the individual shipper for the additional services after 30 days from delivery. If the individual shipper does not agree to pay the additional services, the carrier should perform only those additional services as are required to complete the delivery, and bill the individual shipper for the additional services after 30 days from delivery, except that you may collect at delivery charges for impracticable operations that do not exceed 15 percent of all other charges due at delivery.

(9) If the individual shipper requests additional services after the bill of lading has been issued, you must inform the individual shipper of the additional charges involved. You may require full payment at destination for these additional services and for 100 percent of the original binding estimate. If applicable, you also may require payment at delivery of charges for impracticable operations (as defined in your carrier tariff) not to exceed 15 percent of all other charges due at delivery. You must bill and collect from the individual shipper any applicable charges not collected at delivery in accordance with subpart H of this part.

(10) Failure to relinquish possession of a shipment upon the individual shipper's offer to pay the binding estimate amount (or, in the case of a partial delivery, a prorated percentage of the binding estimate as set forth in paragraph (a)(11) of this section) plus charges for any additional services requested by the shipper after the bill of lading has been issued and charges, if applicable, for impracticable operations (subject to a maximum amount as set forth in paragraph 9 of this section), constitutes a failure to transport a shipment with "reasonable dispatch" and subjects you to cargo delay claims pursuant to part 370 of this chapter.

(11) If you make only a partial delivery of the shipment, you may not demand upon delivery full payment of the binding estimate. You may demand only a prorated percentage of the binding estimate. The prorated percentage must be the percentage of the weight of that portion of the shipment

delivered relative to the total weight of the shipment. For example, if you deliver only 2,500 pounds of a shipment weighing 5,000 pounds, you may demand payment at destination for only 50 percent of the binding estimate.

(b) In accordance with §375.401(a), you may impose a charge for providing a written binding estimate. If you do not provide a binding estimate to an individual shipper, you must provide a non-binding estimate in accordance with §375.405.

(c) You must retain a copy of the binding estimate for each move you perform for at least one year from the date you made the estimate and keep it as an attachment to be made an integral part of the bill of lading contract.

§375.405 How must I provide a non-binding estimate?

(a) If you do not provide a binding estimate to an individual shipper in accordance with §375.403, you must provide a non-binding written estimate to the individual shipper.

(b) If you provide a non-binding estimate to an individual shipper, you must provide your reasonably accurate estimate of the approximate costs the individual shipper should expect to pay for the transportation and services of the shipment. You must comply with the following ten requirements:

(1) You must provide reasonably accurate non-binding estimates based upon both the estimated weight or volume of the shipment and services required and the physical survey of the household goods, if required. If you provide a shipper with an estimate based on volume that will later be converted to a weight-based rate, you must provide the shipper an explanation in writing of the formula used to calculate the conversion to weight.

(2) You must explain to the individual shipper that final charges calculated for shipments moved on non-binding estimates will be those appearing in your tariffs applicable to the transportation. You must explain that these final charges may exceed the approximate costs appearing in your estimate.

(3) You must furnish non-binding estimates without charge and in writing to the individual shipper or other person responsible for payment of the freight charges.

(4) You must retain a copy of each non-binding estimate as an attachment to be made an integral part of the bill of lading contract.

(5) You must clearly indicate on the face of a non-binding estimate that the estimate is not binding upon you and the charges shown are the approximate charges to be assessed for the service identified in the estimate. The estimate must clearly state that the shipper will not be required to pay more than 110 percent of the non-binding estimate at the time of delivery.

(6) You must clearly describe on the face of a non-binding estimate the entire shipment and all services you are providing.

(7) If it appears an individual shipper has tendered additional household goods or requires additional services not identified in the non-binding estimate, you are not required to honor the estimate. If an agreement cannot be reached as to the price or service requirements for the additional goods or services, you are not required to service the shipment. However, if you do service the shipment, before loading the shipment, you must do one of the following two things:

(i) Reaffirm your non-binding estimate.

(ii) Negotiate a revised written non-binding estimate accurately listing, in detail, the additional household goods or services.

(8) Once you load a shipment, failure to execute a new non-binding estimate signifies you have reaffirmed the original non-binding estimate. You may not collect more than 110 percent of the amount of the original non-binding estimate at destination, except as provided in paragraphs (b)(9) and (10) of this section.

(9) If you believe additional services are necessary to properly service a shipment after the bill of lading has been issued, you must inform the individual shipper what the additional services are before performing those services. You must allow the shipper at least one hour to determine whether he or she wants the additional services performed. If the individual shipper agrees to pay for the

additional services, you must execute a written attachment to be made an integral part of the bill of lading contract and have the individual shipper sign the written attachment. This may be done through fax transmissions; e-mail; overnight courier; or certified mail, return receipt requested. You must bill the individual shipper for the additional services after 30 days from delivery. If the individual shipper does not agree to pay the additional services, the carrier should perform only those additional services as are required to complete the delivery, and bill the individual shipper for the additional services after 30 days from delivery, except that you may collect at delivery charges for impracticable operations that do not exceed 15 percent of all other charges due at delivery.

(10) If the individual shipper requests additional services after the bill of lading has been issued, you must inform the individual shipper of the additional charges involved. You may require full payment at destination for these additional services and (unless you make only a partial delivery, in which case you must collect a prorated percentage of the original non-binding estimate as set forth in §375.407(c) of this part) for up to 110 percent of the original non-binding estimate. If applicable, you also may require payment at delivery of charges for impracticable operations (as defined in your carrier tariff) not to exceed 15 percent of all other charges due at delivery. You must bill and collect from the individual shipper any applicable charges not collected at delivery in accordance with subpart H of this part.

(c) If you furnish a non-binding estimate, you must enter the estimated charges upon the order for service and upon the bill of lading.

(d) You must retain a copy of the non-binding estimate for each move you perform for at least one year from the date you made the estimate and keep it as an attachment to be made an integral part of the bill of lading contract.

§375.407 Under what circumstances must I relinquish possession of a collect-on-delivery shipment transported under a non-binding estimate?

(a) If an individual shipper pays you up to 110 percent of the non-binding estimate on a collect-on-delivery shipment (or, in the case of a partial delivery, a prorated percentage of the non-binding estimate as set forth in paragraph (c) of this section), you must relinquish possession of the shipment at the time of delivery. If there are either charges for any additional services requested by the shipper after the bill of lading has been issued and/or charges, if applicable, for impracticable operations (subject to a maximum amount as set forth in paragraph (d) of this section), and the shipper also pays you for such charges, you must relinquish possession of the shipment at the time of delivery. You must accept the form of payment agreed to at the time of estimate, unless the shipper agrees in writing to a change in the form of payment.

(b) Failure to relinquish possession of a shipment after the individual shipper offers to pay you up to 110 percent of the approximate costs of a non-binding estimate plus any additional charges described in paragraph (a) of this section constitutes a failure to transport a shipment with "reasonable dispatch" and subjects you to cargo delay claims pursuant to part 370 of this chapter.

(c) If you make only a partial delivery of the shipment, you may not demand full payment of the non-binding estimate. You may demand at delivery only a prorated percentage of the non-binding estimate (or a prorated percentage of an amount up to 110 percent of the non-binding estimate). The prorated percentage must be the percentage of the weight of that portion of the shipment delivered relative to the total weight of the shipment. For example, if you deliver only 2,500 pounds of a shipment weighing 5,000 pounds, you may demand payment of 50 percent of not more than 110 percent of the non-binding estimate.

(d) You may not demand payment of charges for impracticable operations, as defined in your tariff, of more than 15 percent of all other charges due at delivery. You must bill and collect from the individual shipper charges for impracticable operations not collected at delivery in accordance with subpart H of this part.

§375.409 May household goods brokers provide estimates?

(a) Subject to the limitations in §371.113(a) of this subchapter, household goods brokers may provide estimates to individual shippers provided there is a written agreement between the broker and you, the motor carrier, adopting the broker's estimate as your own estimate. If you, the motor carrier, make such an agreement with a household goods broker, you must ensure compliance with all requirements of this part pertaining to estimates, including the requirement that you must relinquish possession of the shipment if the shipper pays you no more than 110 percent of a non-binding estimate at the time of delivery.

(b) Your written agreement with the household goods broker(s) must include the items required in §371.115(a) of this subchapter.

Subpart E
Pick Up of Shipments of Household Goods

§375.501 Must I write up an order for service?

(a) Before you receive a shipment of household goods you will move for an individual shipper, you must prepare an order for service. The order for service must contain the information described in the following 15 items:

(1) Your name and address and the FMCSA U.S. DOT number assigned to the mover who is responsible for performing the service.

(2) The individual shipper's name, address, and, if available, telephone number(s).

(3) The name, address, and telephone number of the delivering mover's office or agent located at or nearest to the destination of the shipment.

(4) A telephone number where the individual shipper/consignee may contact you or your designated agent.

(5) One of the following three entries must be on the order for service:

(i) The agreed pickup date and agreed delivery date of the move.

(ii) The agreed period(s) of the entire move.

(iii) If you are transporting the shipment on a guaranteed service basis, the guaranteed dates or periods for pickup, transportation, and delivery. You must enter any penalty or per diem requirements upon the agreement under this item.

(6) The names and addresses of any other motor carriers, when known, who will participate in interline transportation of the shipment.

(7) The form of payment you and your agents will honor at delivery. The payment information must be the same that was entered on the estimate.

(8) The terms and conditions for payment of the total charges, including notice of any minimum charges.

(9) The maximum amount you will demand at the time of delivery to obtain possession of the shipment, when you transport on a collect-on-delivery basis.

(10) A statement of the declared value of the shipment, which is the maximum amount of your liability to the individual shipper under your Full Value Protection for the replacement value of any household goods that are lost, damaged, destroyed, or otherwise not delivered to the final destination. If the individual shipper waives, in writing, your Full Value Protection liability, you must include a copy of the waiver; the Surface Transportation Board's required released rates valuation statement; and the charges, if any, for optional valuation coverage (other than Full Value Protection). The released rates may be increased annually by the motor carrier based on the U.S. Department of Commerce's Cost of Living Adjustment.

(11) A complete description of any special or accessorial services ordered and minimum weight or volume charges applicable to the shipment, subject to the following two conditions:

(i) If you provide service for individual shippers on rates based upon the transportation of a minimum weight or volume, you must indicate on the order for service the minimum weight- or volume-based rates, and the minimum charges applicable to the shipment.

(ii) If you do not indicate the minimum rates and charges, your tariff must provide you will compute the final charges relating to such a shipment based upon the actual weight or volume of the shipment.

(12) Any identification or registration number you assign to the shipment.

(13) *For non-binding estimates,* your reasonably accurate estimate of the amount of the charges, the method of payment of total charges, and the maximum amount (no more than 110 percent of the non-binding estimate) you will demand at the time of delivery to relinquish possession of the shipment.

(14) *For binding estimates,* the amount of charges you will demand based upon the binding estimate and the terms of payment under this estimate.

(15) Whether the individual shipper requests notification of the charges before delivery. The individual shipper must provide you with the fax number(s) or address(es) where you will transmit the notifications by fax transmission; e-mail; overnight courier; or certified mail, return receipt requested.

(b) You, your agent, or your driver must inform the individual shipper if you reasonably expect a special or accessorial service is necessary to safely transport a shipment. You must refuse to accept the shipment when you reasonably expect a special or accessorial service is necessary to safely transport a shipment and the individual shipper refuses to purchase the special or accessorial service. You must make a written note if the shipper refuses any special or accessorial services that you reasonably expect to be necessary.

(c) You and the individual shipper must sign the order for service. You must provide a dated copy of the order for service to the individual shipper at the time you sign the order.

(d) (1) You may provide the individual shipper with blank or incomplete estimates, orders for service, bills of lading, or any other blank or incomplete documents pertaining to the move.

(2) You may require the individual shipper to sign an incomplete document at origin provided it contains all relevant shipping information except the actual shipment weight and any other information necessary to determine the final charges for all services performed.

(e) You must provide the individual shipper the opportunity to rescind the order for service without any penalty for a three-day period after the shipper signs the order for service, if the shipper scheduled the shipment to be loaded more than three days after signing the order.

(f) Before loading the shipment, and upon mutual agreement of both you and the individual shipper, you may amend an order for service.

(g) You must retain a copy of the order for service for each move you perform for at least one year from the date you made the order for service and keep it as an attachment to be made an integral part of the bill of lading contract.

(h) You have the option of placing the valuation statement on either the order for service or the bill of lading, provided the order for service or bill of lading states the appropriate valuation selected by the shipper.

§375.503 Must I write up an inventory?

(a) You must prepare a written, itemized inventory for each shipment of household goods you transport for an individual shipper. The inventory must identify every carton and every uncartoned item that is included in the shipment. When you prepare the inventory, an identification number that corresponds to the inventory must be placed on each article that is included in the shipment.

(b) You must prepare the inventory before or at the time of loading in the vehicle for transportation in a manner that provides the individual shipper with the opportunity to observe and verify the accuracy of the inventory if he or she so requests.

(c) You must furnish a complete copy of the inventory to the individual shipper before or at the time of loading the shipment. A copy of the inventory, signed by both you and the individual shipper, must be provided to the shipper, together with a copy of the bill of lading, before or at the time you load the shipment.

(d) Upon delivery, you must provide the individual shipper with the opportunity to observe and verify that the same articles are being delivered and the condition of those articles. You must also provide the individual shipper the opportunity to note in writing any missing articles and the condition of any damaged or destroyed articles. In addition, you must also provide the shipper with a copy of all such notations.

(e) You must retain inventories for each move you perform for at least one year from the date you made the inventory and keep it as an attachment to be made an integral part of the bill of lading contract.

§375.505 Must I write up a bill of lading?

(a) You must issue a bill of lading. The bill of lading must contain the terms and conditions of the contract. A bill of lading may be combined with an order for service to include all the items required by §375.501 of this subpart. You must furnish a partially complete copy of the bill of lading to the individual shipper before the vehicle leaves the residence at origin. The partially complete bill of lading must contain all relevant shipment information, except the actual shipment weight and any other information necessary to determine the final charges for all services performed.

(b) On a bill of lading, you must include the following 14 items:

(1) Your name and address, or the name and address of the motor carrier issuing the bill of lading.

(2) The names and addresses of any other motor carriers, when known, who will participate in transportation of the shipment.

(3) The name, address, and telephone number of your office (or the office of your agent) where the

individual shipper can contact you in relation to the transportation of the shipment.

(4) The form of payment you and your agents will honor at delivery. The payment information must be the same that was entered on the estimate and order for service.

(5) When you transport on a collect-on-delivery basis, the name, address, and if furnished, the telephone number, facsimile number, or e-mail address of a person to notify about the charges. The notification may also be made by overnight courier or certified mail, return receipt requested.

(6) *For non-guaranteed service,* the agreed date or period of time for pickup of the shipment and the agreed date or period of time for the delivery of the shipment. The agreed dates or periods for pickup and delivery entered upon the bill of lading must conform to the agreed dates or periods of time for pickup and delivery entered upon the order for service or a proper amendment to the order for service.

(7) *For guaranteed service,* subject to tariff provisions, the dates for pickup and delivery, and any penalty or per diem entitlements due the individual shipper under the agreement.

(8) The actual date of pickup.

(9) The company or carrier identification number of the vehicle(s) upon which you load the individual shipper's shipment.

(10) The terms and conditions for payment of the total charges, including notice of any minimum charges.

(11) The maximum amount you will demand at the time of delivery to obtain possession of the shipment, when you transport under a collect-on-delivery basis.

(12) The valuation statement provided in the Surface Transportation Board's released rates order requires individual shippers either to choose Full Value Protection for your liability or waive the Full Value Protection in favor of the STB's released rates. The released rates may be increased annually by the motor carrier based on the U.S. Department of Commerce's Cost of Living Adjustment. Contact the STB for a copy of the Released Rates of

Motor Carrier Shipments of Household Goods. If the individual shipper waives your Full Value Protection in writing on the STB's valuation statement, you must include the charges, if any, for optional valuation coverage (other than Full Value Protection).

(13) Evidence of any insurance coverage sold to or procured for the individual shipper from an independent insurer, including the amount of the premium for such insurance.

(14) Each attachment to the bill of lading. Each attachment is an integral part of the bill of lading contract. If not provided elsewhere to the shipper, the following three items must be added as an attachment to the bill of lading.

(i) The binding or non-binding estimate.

(ii) The order for service.

(iii) The inventory.

(c) A copy of the bill of lading must accompany a shipment at all times while in your (or your agent's) possession. Before the vehicle leaves the residence of origin, the bill of lading must be in the possession of the driver responsible for the shipment.

(d) You must retain bills of lading for each move you perform for at least one year from the date you created the bill of lading.

§375.507 Must I determine the weight of a shipment?

(a) When you transport household goods on a non-binding estimate dependent upon the shipment weight, you must determine the weight of each shipment transported before the assessment of any charges.

(b) You must weigh the shipment upon a certified scale.

(c) You must provide a written explanation of volume to weight conversions, when you provide an estimate by volume and convert the volume to weight.

§375.509 How must I determine the weight of a shipment?

(a) You must weigh the shipment by using one of the following two methods:

(1) *First method—origin weigh.* You determine the difference between the tare weight of the vehicle before loading at the origin of the shipment and the gross weight of the same vehicle after loading the shipment.

(2) *Second method—back weigh.* You determine the difference between the gross weight of the vehicle with the shipment loaded and the tare weight of the same vehicle after you unload the shipment.

(b) The following three conditions must exist for both the tare and gross weighings:

(1) The vehicle must have installed or loaded all pads, dollies, hand trucks, ramps, and other equipment required in the transportation of the shipment.

(2) The driver and other persons must be off the vehicle at the time of either weighing.

(3) The fuel tanks on the vehicle must be full at the time of each weighing, or, in the alternative, when you use the *first method—origin weigh,* in paragraph (a)(1) of this section, where the tare weighing is the first weighing performed, you must refrain from adding fuel between the two weighings.

(c) You may detach the trailer of a tractor-trailer vehicle combination from the tractor and have the trailer weighed separately at each weighing provided the length of the scale platform is adequate to accommodate and support the entire trailer at one time.

(d) You must use the net weight of shipments transported in containers. You must calculate the difference between the tare weight of the container (including all pads, blocking and bracing used in the transportation of the shipment) and the gross weight of the container with the shipment loaded in the container.

§375.511 May I use an alternative method for shipments weighing 3,000 pounds or less?

For shipments weighing 3,000 pounds or less (1,362 kilograms or less), you may weigh the shipment upon a platform or warehouse certified scale before loading for transportation or after unloading.

§375.513 Must I give the individual shipper an opportunity to observe the weighing?

You must give the individual shipper or any other person responsible for the payment of the freight charges the right to observe all weighings of the shipment. You must advise the individual shipper, or any other person entitled to observe the weighings, where and when each weighing will occur. You must give the person who will observe the weighings a reasonable opportunity to be present to observe the weighings.

§375.515 May an individual shipper waive his/her right to observe each weighing?

(a) If an individual shipper elects not to observe a weighing, the shipper is presumed to have waived that right.

(b) If an individual shipper elects not to observe a reweighing, the shipper must waive that right in writing. The individual shipper may send the waiver notification via fax transmission; e-mail; overnight courier; or certified mail, return receipt requested.

(c) Waiver of the right to observe a weighing or re-weighing does not affect any other rights of the individual shipper under this part or otherwise.

§375.517 May an individual shipper demand re-weighing?

After you inform the individual shipper of the billing weight and total charges and before actually beginning to unload a shipment weighed at origin (*first method* under §375.509(a)(1)), the individual shipper may demand a re-weigh. You must base your freight bill charges upon the re-weigh weight.

§375.519 Must I obtain weight tickets?

(a) You must obtain weight tickets whenever we require you to weigh the shipment in accordance with this subpart. You must obtain a separate weight ticket for each weighing. The weigh master must sign each weight ticket. Each weight ticket must contain the following six items:

(1) The complete name and location of the scale.

(2) The date of each weighing.

(3) The identification of the weight entries as being the tare, gross, or net weights.

(4) The company or carrier identification of the vehicle.

(5) The last name of the individual shipper as it appears on the bill of lading.

(6) The carrier's shipment registration or bill of lading number.

(b) When both weighings are performed on the same scale, one weight ticket may be used to record both weighings.

(c) As part of the file on the shipment, you must retain the original weight ticket or tickets relating to the determination of the weight of a shipment.

(d) All freight bills you present to an individual shipper must include true copies of all weight tickets obtained in the determination of the shipment weight in order to collect any shipment charges dependent upon the weight transported.

§375.521 What must I do if an individual shipper wants to know the actual weight or charges for a shipment before I tender delivery?

(a) If an individual shipper of a shipment being transported on a collect-on-delivery basis specifically requests notification of the actual weight or volume and charges on the shipment, you must comply with this request. This requirement is conditioned upon the individual shipper's supplying you with an address or telephone number where the individual shipper will receive the communication. You must make your notification by telephone; in person; fax transmissions; e-mail; overnight courier; or certified mail, return receipt requested.

(b) The individual shipper must receive your notification at least one full 24-hour day before any tender of the shipment for delivery, excluding Saturdays, Sundays and Federal holidays.

(c) You may disregard the 24-hour notification requirement on shipments in any one of the following three circumstances:

(1) The shipment will be back weighed (*i.e.*, weighed at destination).

(2) Pickup and delivery encompass two consecutive weekdays, if the individual shipper agrees.

(3) The shipment is moving under a non-binding estimate and the maximum payment required at time of delivery is 110 percent of the estimated charges, but only if the individual shipper agrees to waive the 24-hour notification requirement.

Subpart F
Transportation of Shipments

§375.601 Must I transport the shipment in a timely manner?

Yes. Transportation in a timely manner is also known as "reasonable dispatch service." You must provide reasonable dispatch service to all individual shippers, except for transportation on the basis of guaranteed pickup and delivery dates.

§375.603 When must I tender a shipment for delivery?

You must tender a shipment for delivery for an individual shipper on the agreed delivery date or within the period specified on the bill of lading. Upon the request or concurrence of the individual shipper, you may waive this requirement.

§375.605 How must I notify an individual shipper of any service delays?

(a) When you are unable to perform either the pickup or delivery of a shipment on the dates or during the periods specified in the order for service and as soon as the delay becomes apparent to you, you must notify the individual shipper of the delay, at your expense, in one of the following six ways:

(1) By telephone.

(2) In person.

(3) Fax transmissions.

(4) E-mail.

(5) Overnight courier.

(6) Certified mail, return receipt requested.

(b) You must advise the individual shipper of the dates or periods you expect to be able to pick up and/or deliver the shipment. You must consider the needs of the individual shipper in your advisement. You also must do the following four things:

(1) You must prepare a written record of the date, time, and manner of notification.

(2) You must prepare a written record of your amended date or period for pick-up or delivery.

(3) You must retain these records as a part of your file on the shipment. The retention period is one year from the date of notification.

(4) You must furnish a copy of the notice to the individual shipper by first class mail or in person if the individual shipper requests a copy of the notice.

§375.607 What must I do if I am able to tender a shipment for final delivery more than 24 hours before a specified date?

(a) You may ask the individual shipper to accept an early delivery date. If the individual shipper does not concur with your request or the individual shipper does not request an early delivery date, you may, at your discretion, place a shipment in storage under your own account and at your own expense in a warehouse located near the destination of the shipment. If you place the shipment in storage, you must comply with paragraph (b) of this section. You may comply with paragraph (c) of this section, at your discretion.

(b) You must immediately notify the individual shipper of the name and address of the warehouse where you place the shipment. You must make and keep a record of your notification as a part of your shipment records. You have responsibility for the shipment under the terms and conditions of the bill of lading. You are responsible for the charges for redelivery, handling, and storage until you make final delivery.

(c) You may limit your responsibility under paragraph (b) of this section up to the agreed delivery date or the first day of the period of time of delivery as specified in the bill of lading.

§375.609 What must I do for shippers who store household goods in transit?

(a) If you are holding goods for storage-in-transit (SIT) and the period of time is about to expire, you must comply with this section.

(b) You must notify the individual shipper, in writing of the following four items:

(1) The date of conversion to permanent storage.

(2) The existence of a nine-month period after the date of conversion to permanent storage when the individual shipper may file claims against you for loss or damage occurring to the goods in transit or during the storage-in-transit period.

(3) The fact your liability is ending.

(4) The fact the individual shipper's property will be subject to the rules, regulations, and charges of the warehouseman.

(c) You must make this notification at least 10 days before the expiration date of either one of the following two periods:

(1) The specified period of time when the goods are to be held in storage.

(2) The maximum period of time provided in your tariff for storage-in-transit.

(d) You must notify the individual shipper by facsimile transmission; e-mail; overnight courier; or certified mail, return receipt requested.

(e) If you are holding household goods in storage-in-transit for a period of time less than 10 days, you must give notification to the individual shipper of the information specified in paragraph (b) of this section one day before the expiration date of the specified time when the goods are to be held in such storage.

(f) You must maintain a record of notifications as part of the records of the shipment.

(g) Your failure or refusal to notify the individual shipper will automatically effect a continuance of your carrier liability according to the applicable tariff provisions with respect to storage-in-transit, until the end of the day following the date when you actually gave notice.

(h) When you place household goods in permanent storage, you must place the household goods in the name of the individual shipper and provide contact information for the shipper in the form of a telephone number, mailing address and/or email address.

Subpart G
Delivery of Shipments

§375.701 May I provide for a release of liability on my delivery receipt?

(a) Your delivery receipt or shipping document must not contain any language purporting to release or discharge you or your agents from liability.

(b) The delivery receipt may include a statement the property was received in apparent good condition except as noted on the shipping documents.

§375.703 What is the maximum collect-on-delivery amount I may demand at the time of delivery?

(a) On a binding estimate, the maximum amount is the exact estimate of the charges, plus charges for any additional services requested by the shipper after the bill of lading has been issued and charges, if applicable, for impracticable operations as defined in your carrier tariff. The maximum amount of charges for impracticable operations you may collect on delivery is an amount equal to 15 percent of all other charges due at delivery.

(b) On a non-binding estimate, the maximum amount is 110 percent of the non-binding estimate of the charges, plus charges for any additional services requested by the shipper after the bill of lading has been issued and charges, if applicable, for impracticable operations as defined in your carrier tariff. The maximum amount of charges for impracticable operations you may collect on delivery is an amount equal to 15 percent of all other charges due at delivery.

§375.705 If a shipment is transported on more than one vehicle, what charges may I collect at delivery?

(a) At your discretion, you may do one of the following three things:

(1) You may defer the collection of all charges until you deliver the entire shipment.

(2) If you have determined the charges for the entire shipment, you may collect charges for the portion of the shipment tendered for delivery. You must determine the percentage of the charges for the entire shipment represented by the portion of the shipment tendered for delivery.

(3) If you cannot reasonably calculate the charges for the entire shipment, you must determine the charges for the portion of the shipment being delivered. You must collect this amount. The total charges you assess for the transportation of the

separate portions of the shipment must not be more than the charges due for the entire shipment.

(b) In the event of the loss or destruction of any part of a shipment transported on more than one vehicle, you must collect the charges as provided in §375.707.

§375.707 If a shipment is partially lost or destroyed, what charges may I collect at delivery?

(a) (1) If a shipment is partially lost or destroyed, you may collect at delivery:

(i) A prorated percentage of the binding estimate or a prorated percentage of up to 110 percent of the non-binding estimate. The prorated percentage is equal to the percentage of the weight of that portion of the shipment delivered relative to the total weight of the shipment. For example, if you deliver only 2,500 pounds of a shipment weighing 5,000 pounds, you may demand at destination, as applicable, only 50 percent of a binding estimate or 50 percent of not more than 110 percent of a non-binding estimate;

(ii) Charges for any additional services requested by the shipper after the bill of lading has been issued; and

(iii) Charges for impracticable operations, if applicable, except that such charges must not exceed 15 percent of all other charges due at delivery.

(iv) Any specific valuation charge due.

(2) You must bill and collect from the individual shipper any remaining charges not collected at delivery in accordance with subpart H of this part.

(b) You must determine, at your own expense, the proportion of the shipment, based on actual or constructive weight, not lost or destroyed in transit.

(c) You may disregard paragraph (a)(1) of this section if loss or destruction was due to an act or omission of the individual shipper.

(d) The individual shipper's rights are in addition to, and not in lieu of, any other rights the individual shipper may have with respect to a shipment of household goods you or your agent(s) partially lost or destroyed in transit. This applies whether or not the individual shipper exercises any rights to obtain a refund of the portion of your published freight charges corresponding to the portion of the lost or destroyed shipment (including any charges for accessorial or terminal services) at the time you dispose of claims for loss, damage, or injury to articles in the shipment under part 370 of this chapter.

§375.709 If a shipment is totally lost or destroyed, what charges may I collect at delivery?

(a) You are forbidden from collecting, or requiring an individual shipper to pay, any freight charges (including any charges for accessorial or terminal services) when a household goods shipment is *totally lost or destroyed* in transit. The following two conditions also apply:

(1) You must collect any specific valuation charge due.

(2) You may disregard paragraph (a) of this section if loss or destruction was due to an act or omission of the individual shipper.

(b) The individual shipper's rights are in addition to, and not in lieu of, any other rights the individual shipper may have with respect to a shipment of household goods you or your agent(s) totally lost or destroyed in transit. This applies whether or not the individual shipper exercises its rights provided in paragraph (a) of this section.

Subpart H
Collection of Charges

§375.801 What types of charges apply to subpart H?

This subpart applies to all shipments of household goods that:

(a) Entail a balance due freight or expense bill, or

(b) Are transported on an extension of credit basis.

§375.803 How must I present my freight or expense bill?

You must present your freight or expense bill in accordance with §375.807 of this subpart.

§375.805 If I am forced to relinquish a collect-on-delivery shipment before the payment of ALL charges, how do I collect the balance?

On "collect-on-delivery" shipments, you must present your freight bill for all transportation charges within 15 days as required by §375.807.

§375.807 What actions may I take to collect the charges upon my freight bill?

(a) You must present a freight bill within 15 days (excluding Saturdays, Sundays, and Federal holidays) of the date of delivery of a shipment at its destination.

(b) The credit period must be seven days (including Saturdays, Sundays, and Federal holidays).

(c) You must provide in your tariffs the following four things:

(1) You must automatically extend the credit period to a total of 30 calendar days for any shipper who has not paid your freight bill within the 7-day period. However, for charges for impracticable operations that are not collected at delivery, you

may not extend the credit period beyond 30 days after you present your freight bill.

(2) You will assess a service charge to each individual shipper equal to one percent of the amount of the freight bill, subject to a $20 minimum charge, for the extension of the credit period. You will assess the service charge for each 30-day extension the charges go unpaid.

(3) You must deny credit to any shipper who fails to pay a duly-presented freight bill within the 30-day period. You may grant credit to the individual shipper when the individual shipper satisfies he/she will promptly pay all future freight bills duly presented.

(4) You must ensure all payments of freight bills are strictly in accordance with the rules and regulations of this part for the settlement of your rates and charges.

Subpart I
Penalties

§375.901 What penalties do we impose for violations of this part?

The penalty provisions of 49 U.S.C. Chapter 149, Civil and Criminal Penalties apply to this part. These penalties do not overlap. Notwithstanding these civil penalties, nothing in this section shall deprive any holder of a receipt or a bill of lading any remedy or right of action under existing law.

Printed in Dunstable, United Kingdom

91220870R10132